Triumph Spitfire and GT6

The Complete Story

Other Titles in the Crowood AutoClassics Series

TRIUMPH SPITFIRE and GT6 *The Complete Story*

James Taylor

First published in 2000 by
The Crowood Press Ltd
Ramsbury, Marlborough
Wiltshire SN8 2HR

British Library Cataloguing-in-Publication Data
A catalogue record for this book is available from the British Library.

ISBN 1 86126 262 0

Acknowledgements
The author would like to thank Graham Robson, Mike Key and Pete Robain for the loan of
photos for use in this book. Thanks also to Tony Beadle and *Triumph World* magazine, and to
The Spitfire Graveyard, Sheffield.

Designed and typeset by Textype Typesetters, Cambridge
Printed and bound by T. J. International, Padstow

Contents

Evolution

Summer 1960	first 'Bomb' prototype constructed
July 1961	Board approval for purchase of production tooling
October 1962	Spitfire 4 introduced
March 1965	Spitfire Mk 2 introduced
October 1966	GT6 introduced
March 1967	Spitfire Mk 3 introduced
September 1968	GT6 Mk 2 and GT6+ introduced
	first Federalized Spitfires for USA
October 1970	Spitfire Mk IV and GT6 Mk 3 introduced
January 1973	Spitfire 1500 version of Mk IV for USA introduced
December 1973	final GT6 built
November 1974	Spitfire 1500 introduced
August 1980	final Spitfire built

1   In the Beginning

The Triumph name is now dead and buried, a casualty of the changes which swept through the British motor industry in the 1960s. These were finally played out in the 1980s when the drastically slimmed down remains of the British Leyland combine created in 1968 were renamed as the Rover Group. So it is important to explain the heritage of the name and to look at the

Harry Webster was the man in charge of Triumph engineering throughout the gestation period of the Spitfire and the GT6; from 1968 he took charge of British Leyland's Austin-Morris division – hence the picture in the background here.

public expectations of a car from the Triumph stable when the Spitfire was announced in 1962.

Triumph's history as a car manufacturer dates back to 1923, but before that the marque was well known as a manufacturer of pedal cycles and motor cycles. Its first four-wheeled products were small cars, but its manager Claude Holbrook was determined to move into the more lucrative middle-class market, and during the 1930s Triumph fielded a range of attractive and quite expensive cars, many of them with sporting pretensions. Despite the excellence of many of its products, however, Triumph always seemed to fall between two stools: the more staid of its models were never quite as good as the sober Rovers, and the more sporting ones were never quite as good as the rakish Rileys and SS Jaguars. Its problems were compounded by a disastrous marketing policy which saw far too many different models on offer at once. The results were high costs and, by the end of the decade, bankruptcy.

The company was bought by a steelmaking group; but before any major changes could be made the Second World War put paid to all car manufacture in Britain. The former Triumph factories were turned over to war work for the government, and in November 1940 were almost totally destroyed in the German bombing of Coventry. This effectively severed all links with the original Triumph company, and so when Sir John Black's Standard company bought the name and the remaining assets in 1944 all that was left was the Triumph

Triumph's post-war sporting reputation had been made by the TR sports cars; the first of these was the TR2, seen here in early production 'long-door' form with the company's competitions manager Ken Richardson at the wheel.

reputation for stylish saloons and sporting tourers.

Black had his own plans for Triumph, and they were to make it an extension of his own company to produce the more glamorous cars for a volatile market while Standard continued to make bread-and-butter machinery for the masses. It was only when MG and Jaguar started to make a killing in the late 1940s by exporting sports two-seaters to the USA that Sir John resolved to use the Triumph name to spearhead his own ambitions in that mar-

ket. His first attempt was a bulbous creation called the Triumph TRX and based on the Standard Vanguard chassis and running-gear. When that failed, and a subsequent plan to take over the Morgan company (which was doing well with Standard-engined two-seaters in the USA) did also, Black decided to have another crack at building a Triumph sports car out of existing Standard components.

The result was known as the 20TS and was finished just in time to be shown at the Earls Court Motor Show in autumn 1952.

Saloons were normally Standard's preserve in the 1950s, although there was an attempt to establish the Triumph name in the market as well; this Mayflower was one of the designs, but it was not a great success.

It was not yet ready for production, but it provoked such a positive reaction that Sir John took some extra trouble to get it right. He engaged Ken Richardson, formerly involved with the BRM Grand Prix car, to test-drive the prototype, and, when Richardson put forward some strong criticisms, he found himself being offered a job at Triumph in charge of developing the car. Much revised, and all the better for it, the Triumph sports car appeared at the Geneva Show in March 1953 under the name of the TR2. It was a huge success and went on to spawn the even more successful

TR3 which was introduced in 1955, and the further improved TR3A of 1957.

During the 1950s, therefore, Triumph's reputation rested on the success of its sports cars. There were Triumph saloons in the post-war period, but the razor-edge 1800/2000 (later Renown) models introduced in 1946 and the strange little Mayflower introduced in 1950 had both gone by 1954 and were not much mourned. For most of the 1950s saloons would be Standard's preserve, while Triumph would concentrate on sports cars.

However, things were not quite as simple

as the Standard-Triumph management might have wished. The company's major market was by this time in the USA, and by the middle of the decade it was planning to try selling its saloons there as well. The main stumbling block was that the Standard name meant absolutely nothing across the Atlantic and that, with its overtones of 'ordinary', it was not likely to set the US market alight. Thus when the Standard Ten saloon was introduced to the USA in 1957 it was rebadged as a Triumph. Even more blatantly trading on the reputation of Triumph's sports cars, it was actually called a TR10!

Whether Standard-Triumph's desire to succeed in the American market was the only reason behind the decision to drop the Standard name altogether is not clear. However, by 1959, when a new small car was introduced to replace the Standard Eight and Ten, the principle must have been established because this was badged as a Triumph Herald. This left only the Standard Atlas van and the Standard Vanguard saloon in production. The Atlas disappeared altogether in 1961; the Vanguard was replaced by the Triumph

Michelotti had also styled the TR4, the version of the TR range which was in production when the Spitfire came on-stream.

Triumph people

After the Leyland takeover of 1961 (and therefore throughout the period of the Spitfire's production), Stanley Markland was put in as Triumph's chairman. However, Markland resigned in 1963 when he was passed over for the chairmanship of Leyland, and in his place came Donald (later Sir Donald) Stokes. The chief executive was George Turnbull, while Harry Webster was the director of engineering.

2000 in 1963, and after that the Standard name was never used again in Britain (although it did appear on several Indian-built cars assembled from CKD kits).

Meanwhile, important changes had been taking place within the engineering department at Standard-Triumph. In 1955 the body stylist Walter Belgrove departed from the company after a disagreement, leaving Standard-Triumph with no expertise in that design area. There is no doubt that Belgrove's loss was keenly felt, and the

The Spitfire was derived from the Herald saloon, of which an early 948cc example is seen here.

Triumph factories

It is well known that the administrative headquarters of Triumph was at Canley, near Coventry, but the company actually owned several factories which were spread over a wide area. The Canley headquarters had belonged to Standard since 1916, and since 1946 its factory buildings had also housed the Triumph production lines. In 1961 a large, new assembly hall had been opened on the site to cope with the new model ranges planned for the decade.

Canley, however, was primarily an assembly plant. During the 1960s the bodies for Triumph cars were actually built at Bordesley Green, where the company owned the factory formerly occupied by Mulliner's of Birmingham and the associated Forward Radiator Company. Body preparation was undertaken at the old Fisher and Ludlow plant in Tile Hill, near Coventry, before delivery to Canley. Suspension and steering components arrived from Alford and Alder, in Hemel Hempstead, while heavy castings came from the old Bean Industries factory at Tipton in Staffordshire and other components from the Radford plant in Coventry, which had been bought from Daimler in 1957.

---

chief engineer Harry Webster has said that the company was struggling to come up with acceptable shapes for its new projects at this period. An American consultant named Carl Otto was engaged to style the 1956 Standard Vanguard III, but a long-term solution was not found until later that year.

It was quite by chance that Standard-Triumph encountered the Italian stylist Giovanni Michelotti. A businessman, Raymond Flower, had approached the company about supplies of mechanical components for a new car – the Frisky – which he wanted to build and sell in Egypt. During the course of a meeting he happened to mention that he knew where he could get cars styled and built in a matter of only two or three months. Harry Webster followed up this lead, and discovered that the swift stylist was Michelotti, who was using Vignale of Turin to turn his ideas into metal.

The managing Director Alick Dick and the general manager Martin Tustin asked Michelotti to draw up a sports car for them and were highly impressed with the 'dream car' he constructed on a TR chassis in time for the Geneva Show in March 1957. Before

long, they had him on a retainer as Triumph's consultant stylist. Over the summer of that year he came up with the styling for the Herald, the small car intended to replace the Standard Eight and the Standard Ten, and which is of particular importance in this story because it was the direct ancestor of the Spitfire sports-car family.

Like all the other vehicle projects on which Standard-Triumph were working in the middle 1950s, the Herald was being developed under a four-letter code name beginning with Z. In this case it was known as Zobo. Webster had already decided that the car would, in effect, take a step backwards from the small Standards by having a separate chassis instead of unitary construction. There were several reasons for this bold step, one of them being that all the big companies capable of making a unitary bodyshell were fully booked for years ahead. However, the most important were that Standard-Triumph planned to export this car in CKD form to its factories in Australia, India and South Africa, and that the company also wanted to develop several model variants on the same platform. Separate-chassis construction certainly made the CKD side of things easier, and it would be much cheaper to have a common chassis for the saloon, estate, coupé, convertible and van models than to have a different monocoque for each one. When the Standard-Triumph board looked at the timing of the Zobo project in August 1957 there was even a mention of a sports-car derivative, although any further consideration of the idea was deferred. It was that idea which, several years later, would develop into the Triumph Spitfire.

Zobo was launched as the Triumph Herald in 1959 and was well received, although there were some early problems with the build quality. At this stage Standard-Triumph were doing very well, but their fortunes were just about to take an unexpected tumble. By the spring of 1960 it was clear that sales were not up to expectations, neither at home nor in the vital American market. In Britain, government measures to control inflation had included higher charges for credit, and the car trade had been hit hard indeed. Triumph posted good end-of-year figures in the summer of 1960, indicating a profit of £1.8 million after tax, but by November the company was in the red.

It was at this time that the truck and bus

The Spitfire was aimed at the market for affordable sports cars, where the Austin Healey Sprite would always be its main competitor.

The Bomb prototypes				
Number	*Registration*	*Build date*	*Engine*	*Remarks*
X659	–	October 1960	X854, 948cc	built in Italy by Michelotti on a modified 948cc Herald coupé chassis
X661	–	late 1960	original engine not known; later had GA 57428, 1,147cc	'mule' development vehicle made from shortened Herald coupé
X691	4305 VC	spring 1962	original engine not known; later had HE18491HE	first proper prototype, later developed into 'GT' (coupé) body prototype; later still used for tests with fuel injection and on exhaust emissions work
X692	412 VC	spring 1962	FC 2 HE, 1,147cc	built with LHD and used for endurance tests; later used for rallies (see Ch. 9)

maker Leyland Motors was looking to expand its business interests and, through its existing contacts with Standard-Triumph, learned of the company's plight. It made a take-over bid in December 1960 and gained control of the company in April 1961 – after a temporary hesitation when the scale of Standard-Triumph's losses became apparent in the early months of 1960 and the company started working a three-day week. When the situation did not improve in line with Standard-Triumph's forecasts, Leyland promptly sacked the company's existing directors and, in August 1961, put in its own man to run the company. Stanley Markland was a highly respected engineer who had already been acting as the Leyland liaison man at Standard-Triumph, and in that role he had already been able to gain agreement for the car which would become the Spitfire to enter production.

In fact, Harry Webster had returned to the idea of a Zobo-based sports car not many months after the Herald had been launched, but his plans had been submerged in the upheaval surrounding the Leyland take-over. As early as April 1960 he had formally proposed such a car to the Standard-Triumph board. He believed that Triumph could and should build a small sports car at a price below that of the existing TR models. The mechanical hardware existed and was already being made for the Herald, and so the cost could be kept low. Moreover, Triumph's reputation as a sports-car manufacturer would more or less guarantee success. BMC was already doing well with the Austin-Healey Sprite, launched in 1958, and there was little doubt in Webster's mind that Triumph could come up with a better product.

The board approved construction of a first prototype for this car – codenamed Bomb – in September 1960. However, by this stage Webster had already set

Looking remarkably like the production model, this is Michelotti's original 'Bomb' prototype, pictured in October 1960; for differences of detail look at the over-riders (taller), the grille (wider spacing of the vertical bars), the bonnet (no central moulding, no badges) and the doors (shallower at the rear, higher door handle).

Michelotti to work on the idea. The Italian had put forward a number of sketches, and the chosen one had been turned into a full-sized, wooden buck on a cut-down Herald chassis. A 948cc Herald coupé then became the donor car for the first running prototype, and the first Bomb – car number X659 in Triumph's experimental series – was delivered to Coventry in October 1960. Unfortunately, by that time financial problems had taken a firm hold on the company and so no further work was done on the pro-

ject. The Bomb prototype was parked in a corner of the Triumph experimental department, covered with a dust-sheet, and forgotten.

It was this prototype which Stanley Markland saw in the early spring of 1961 when he was being shown around the department by Harry Webster. He liked it at once and told Webster that he should go ahead and prepare it for production. He meant what he said too, and on 13 July 1961 the Bomb project was approved for production.

The production Spitfire 4

The backbone chassis of the production Spitfire was similar to that of the Herald models, but lacked its rearward extensions and the perimeter sections to which the saloon's body was mounted. In addition, the two box-sections were more widely spaced, allowing the primary exhaust silencer to be mounted in a protected position between them. There were two short, body-mounting brackets on each side of the 'backbone', and the whole frame terminated at a stiffened cross-member directly behind the axle. The final drive and the dampers were bolted to this.

The body was made entirely of steel, with a forward-hinged front-end section which afforded excellent access to the engine. The hinged boot lid gave access to a reasonably capacious boot, although painted metal sidewalls, the scissors jack mounted on the left-hand side and the exposed fuel tank were not always kind to soft luggage, and the spare wheel sat on the boot floor where it could also deposit dirt on anything carried nearby.

The soft top – there was no hardtop option at first – was not permanently attached to the car but had to be built up when needed. Its tubular frame was stored in the boot behind the fuel tank when not in use, and its PVC covering folded neatly into a well behind the seats, which was otherwise used for light luggage and parcels. A PVC cover could be fitted over this well, and was held in place by press-stud fasteners. There was naturally no question of a rear seat: the Spitfire was an uncompromising two-seater, with thinly-padded bucket seats for the driver and the passenger. These had tilting backrests to give access to the rear compartment, and their cushions could be moved over a range of 7.5in (190mm) fore and aft and locked in any one of twelve positions to suit drivers of different heights.

Among the car's more unusual features were the winding windows in the doors at a time when many sports cars still relied on fabric sidescreens. These did make the doors quite thick, which in turn compromised the interior width of the cockpit. Instruments were arranged in the middle of the dashboard to allow the same dashboard pressing to be used for both left-hand- and right-hand-drive cars, and the dashboard was visibly braced to the floor on either side of the transmission tunnel in the way pioneered on the TR models in order to prevent scuttle shake. For competition use, the windscreen frame could be removed in its entirety by undoing three fixing bolts.

The steering wheel and column controls were Triumph Herald items and the rake of the column could be adjusted by undoing a clamp on its support bracket below the dash, while the wheel could also be moved over a range of 4in (102mm) in the horizontal plane by undoing a locking bolt. As with the Herald's, the Spitfire's steering column was designed to collapse on impact. The gear lever was cranked rearwards to suit its forward positioning on the transmission tunnel, and there was a 'fly-off' type of handbrake (which was released by pulling upwards and locked on by depressing a button at the end of the handle). A heater was available – but at an extra cost – and there was carpet material only on the transmission tunnel. On the floor were rubber mats.

The 1,147cc engine was an uprated Herald 1200 unit, with bigger valves and a higher compression ratio, twin SU carburettors replacing the saloon's single Solex, a camshaft borrowed from the twin-carburettor 948cc Herald coupé engine, and a cast-iron exhaust manifold with improved gas flow characteristics. It put out 63bhp at 5,750rpm and 67 lb.ft of torque at 3,500rpm. This compared with the 41bhp at 4,600rpm and 61 lb.ft at 2,250rpm of the Herald 1200 engine. The Herald's Lucas distributor was also replaced by an AC Delco type with an integral take-off for the rev counter which the saloon, of course, did not have.

The gearbox was borrowed in its entirety from the Herald 1200, and lacked synchromesh on bottom gear. There was no overdrive at first. The 4.11:1 final drive was also from the Herald, and the front and the rear suspension were of the Herald type, but with different spring and damper rates to suit the lighter car and its different weight distibution. Steering was the Herald's rack-and-pinion type, and the Spitfire boasted an even tighter turning circle (24ft 2in/7.37m) than the Herald's already astonishing 25ft (7.62m).

As for the brakes, once again the Herald's system was used, although the standard 7in (178mm) rear drums were matched as standard on the Spitfire by the Herald's optional disc brakes.

Many engineering decisions still had to be made at this stage, however. In April 1960 the Standard-Triumph board had havered between using steel or GRP for the bodyshell, no doubt mindful of the recent difficulties there had been in getting a supplier for the Herald's body. By the summer of 1961 it was clear that the body would be made by the Forward Radiator Company, and that meant that it would have steel panels. (GRP bodies were still relatively new in Britain at this period and few companies had the expertise to make them.) With a steel body it would be possible to have strong sills to give the necessary rigidity, so that the perimeter frames of the Herald's chassis would not be needed. Instead, Webster decided on a strong backbone-frame chassis, flared out at the front

to support the engine. This was similar in its general concept to the central part of the Herald chassis; but, of course, it had no cross-members. This in turn led to a small change in the rear suspension, which had to be attached to the bodyshell of the Bomb, while on the Herald it was mounted to a chassis cross-member.

The chassis differed from the Herald's in yet another regard, because right from the start of the Bomb project in 1960 Harry Webster had decided that the two-seater sports car's wheelbase should be 8.5in (216mm) shorter than the four-seater saloon's at 83in (2,108mm). The same basic suspension layout was retained both front and rear, the front having twin wishbones with coil springs and an anti-roll bar, and the rear being a crude, independent type

The Triumph 2000 saloon was also Michelotti's work; this is a 1967 car, one of the last of the Mk I models.

with swing-axles and a single transverse leaf spring bolted to the top of the differential casing. This rear suspension was simple and cheap to make, but it would prove to be one of the weak points of the Spitfire and of its later and more powerful GT6 derivative. The Herald never had enough performance to show up the inherent handling deficiencies of the layout, but the sports cars did.

The early Heralds had drum brakes all round, but Webster decided to fit disc brakes to the sports car's front wheels. The TR models already had them and so it would continue a Triumph tradition; but perhaps more significant was that the Austin-Healey Sprite did not. Fitting discs to the Bomb would give the Triumph an edge in the sales race which was bound to ensue. The Herald's rack-and-pinion steering already gave the sharp handling needed in a sports car and so was retained. As for the engine, the 948cc Herald type was not really going to give the necessary

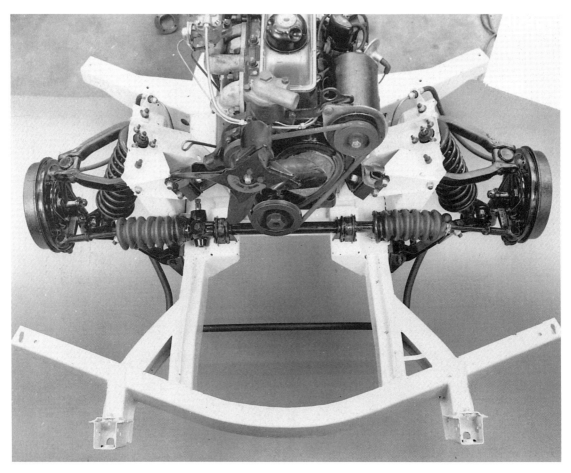

This fascinating photograph was taken on 9 March 1962 and shows the first of the prototype Spitfires (X691) under construction; the engine is a 'slave' unit – and those drum brakes would not be carried through to production.

performance, even when fitted with the optional twin carburettors. However, a big-bore, 1,147cc version of the engine (with the bores repositioned in the block as well) was under development for the Herald, and fitting this with twin carburettors would most certainly give the sort of performance Webster had in mind.

Many of these elements were built into a 'mule' prototype which bore the experimental identification number X661. This car was built in 1960 and, to the casual observer, looked like a 948cc Herald coupé painted in an uninspired shade of grey. That colour was a deliberate choice, of course, to deflect attention from what was really a Bomb development car. A closer look would have revealed that the car had been 'cut-and-shut' so that it rode on the 83in wheelbase intended for the sports car. Later it also ran an 1,147cc engine (number GA 57428).

There was further body development necessary as well, but this could not be done on the short-wheelbase Herald coupé. The Triumph engineers had to work out a

412 VC was the second Triumph-built Bomb prototype, with experimental commission number X692; it was constructed in the spring of 1962.

way of turning the hand-built Michelotti body into a mass-produced production type, and this involved much more work than was visible on the final result. While they would no doubt have wished to incorporate as many existing body sections as possible to save costs, they ended up by using only three. One of those – the TR4 windscreen – had already been incorporated in Michelotti's original. The other two were the inner rear wheelarches, which were shared with the Herald 1200 saloon.

Yet the production body shell had lost none of the prettiness of Michelotti's original, and Triumph had made few visual changes. The Herald-type, forward-hinged front end was again something on the Michelotti original, and was no doubt designed into that because of its great success on the Herald. Its hinges were neatly concealed by the front over-riders, which Triumph reduced in size for the production models. More radical was the change to the dashboard, where Michelotti's typically Italian cluster of three dials in a pod directly ahead of the driver was replaced by a full-width facia panel with the dials grouped in the centre. This again was done to reduce costs and it allowed the same basic dashboard to be used for both the left-hand- and the right-hand-drive versions. In addition, Harry Webster wanted to incorporate winding door-windows to give the Triumph an edge over the Austin-Healey Sprite, and to allow for this the height of the doors had to be increased slightly.

The next prototypes were not completed until the spring of 1962, which makes clear how much engineering development had to be put in after the board had given the Bomb project its approval in July 1961. Every bit as attractive as their Italian-built predecessor, they were numbered as X691 and X692, and registered as 4305 VC and 412 VC, respectively. Over the summer of 1962 they went through the usual punishing routine of endurance and pavé testing, and by autumn Triumph were satisfied with the results. It was just as well; the new sports car, now bearing the name Spitfire, was scheduled to be launched at the Earls Court Motor Show during October.

2 Spitfire 4 (1962–65) and Spitfire Mk 2 (1965–67)

The first time most people saw the new Spitfire 4 was on the Triumph stand at the Earls Court Motor Show which opened on 17 October 1962. Alongside examples of the TR4, the Vitesse and the Herald 1200 in the saloon and the estate form on Stand 122 were two examples of the new car. On the turntable was a white car with blue trim and a black hood, and on the floor was a signal red car with black upholstery and a black hood. The white had the optional extra of whitewall tyres.

The Spitfire took pride of place on the Earls Court Show stand when it was introduced in 1962 as a 1963 model; the white car is on a revolving turntable and the car in the foreground is finished in Signal Red with a black interior.

It would have been difficult not to admit that the new car looked quite stunning. Its flowing Michelotti lines made the obvious domestic competitors – the Austin-Healey Sprite and the MG Midget – look quite dumpy by comparison, and its higher price tag was easily justified by the level of its standard equipment. By this stage, however, only tiny numbers of Spitfires had actually been made at Triumph's Canley works, and the customers who flocked to place orders had to wait their turn. Production gradually built up towards the end of 1962, but only 1,289 cars had been assembled by the end of December and January 1963 would be the first month of full production, when more than 1,250 came off the lines. All these first cars were destined for the home market, where Triumph could keep an eye on them and see whether any problems developed. Exports began early in 1963, when the company was satisfied that it was not going to be flooded with expensive warranty claims from far-flung parts of the world.

WHAT THE BRITISH PRESS SAID

When *The Motor* reported on a Spitfire registered 3609 VC in its issue dated 7 November 1962, its staff were full of enthusiasm for the new car. 'An outstanding new small sports car', they said, which 'will appeal equally as a comfortable road car and useful competition mount.' They thought that its 'first class gear change and almost faultless disc brakes ensure a strong appeal to the keen and skilful sporting driver' and wrote glowingly of its 'exemplary all-weather equipment including winding windows which influence the car's character very strongly.' The car's ride was also excellent, and there was enough

seat adjustment to cope with the needs of a 6ft 4in (1.93m) driver.

This barrage of praise would have been enough to persuade any buyer in the market for a small sports car in late 1962 that he had to give serious consideration to the new Spitfire. Yet the report was not without criticism. The testers found the car's cockpit rather narrow, the interior trim verging on the spartan, the seats insufficiently supportive of thighs and the central instruments poorly placed because they were often obscured by the driver's hand. There was plenty of noise to contend with, from the unsilenced carburettor air intakes and the deep exhaust, and the engine was a bit rough when pulling hard. The gear ratios were not ideal and were too widely spaced for a sports car; in particular, there was a big gap between second and third.

The original cross-hatched grille was seen only on the Mk 1 cars.

Synchromesh on bottom gear would also have been welcome.

The Motor staff also spotted the Spitfire's biggest handling weakness – its tendency to snap suddenly into oversteer when the swing-axle rear suspension jacked up under heavy cornering, the wheels tucked under and the tyres lost their grip. However, they played this down, pulling punches about the failings of a domestic product, as was the custom of the time.

Handling overall was described as 'safe and enjoyable', and the transition to oversteer was described as a gentle one. They pointed out that to increase the tyre pressures to 23psi at the front and 28psi at the rear (the factory recommendations were 18 and 24psi, respectively) did improve the handling, but not the traction from the Dunlop C41 crossply tyres.

When John Bolster of *Autosport* tested a car for that magazine's issue of 11 January

The original dashboard looked particularly attractive when the matt black of the instrument surround and the grab handle contrasted with a lighter body colour; this is the original, two-spoke, Herald-style steering wheel; no radio was fitted to this car and so the aperture ahead of the gear lever is covered by a blanking plate.

1963, he was equally lavish with his praise. For him, the Spitfire was 'a most exciting new, small sports car', and he was particularly impressed by its high level of appointments and its refinement:

> It is quite remarkable what a sense of luxury this convertible body gives, and it is in no way inferior to a conventional saloon in this respect. These creature comforts do not make the little machine any less sporting, and with the hood down the appearance is as dashing as the most avid enthusiast could wish.

All things are relative, of course, and Bolster's enthusiasm for the Spitfire's creature comforts needs to be judged in the knowledge that sports cars of the 1960s were not generally very well-equipped!

Autosport liked the fly-off handbrake and the flexible engine. The cockpit gave insufficient shoulder and elbow room for the driver, though, and an oil-pressure

Early Spitfire seats were shaped to resemble racing 'buckets' and were piped in a contrasting colour; comfort was not a strong point!

gauge would have been an improvement. The ride was firm and, as for the handling, the car would oversteer only if hurled into a corner, when it would remain fully controllable. Again, that comment is better understood with the knowledge that Bolster was a much more experienced driver than most of the Spitfire's buyers would ever be...

SPITFIRE 4 REACHES THE USA

The first Spitfires reached the USA in the early months of 1963. Triumph eagerly awaited customer reactions, because the car's success across the Atlantic was an important factor in its viability, and a failure would have reflected badly on the existing Triumph models which at this stage were selling strongly. However, the Spitfire 4 which went on sale in the USA made only two concessions to American tastes and requirements: it had left-hand drive and it was supplied with whitewall tyres. The days when American Spitfires would need to be quite different from those for the rest of the world were still a long way off.

Triumph need hardly have worried, because the Americans fell for the Spitfire straight away. Nevertheless, they quickly discovered its tail-happy handling, and before long Triumph dealers were marketing a bolt-on camber compensator for the rear axle as an optional extra. This appears to have been designed and manufactured in the USA and was ostensibly a competition extra. It consisted of a bar which bolted between the rear hubs and ran under the axle, thus limiting the amount by which the rear wheels could tuck under in cornering.

WHAT THE AMERICAN PRESS SAID

The Spitfire was acclaimed across the Atlantic, and road test reports published by three of the leading magazines of the time make clear what the Americans found so attractive about Triumph's newest model. *Car and Driver* published its report in March 1963 and *Motor Trend* followed suit in December. Then in June 1965, just as the Mk 2 models were about to be introduced, *Auto Topics* belatedly tested a car.

Car and Driver thought that the Spitfire was 'a more practical car for everyday use than anything we have so far seen in this size', and that it had 'more to offer than was promised by its appearance.' So good was it, in fact, that the magazine's testers thought the Spitfire had 'a good chance to take over the position as Triumph's best-selling model in the US market.'

The high torque developed by the engine at low revs combined with the light weight of the car to give unusual flexibility, and *Car and Driver* thought the engine was also remarkably silent. There was praise for the light and neutral-feeling rack and pinion steering, but – somehow – the magazine failed to pick up the swing axles' ability to provoke sudden oversteer in hard cornering. Perhaps the testers did not drive the car hard enough. They did, however, find other areas to criticize. The car was sensitive to side winds, and the combination of limited wheel travel and hard springing led to a harsh ride on rough roads. The Dunlop C41 crossply tyres also showed their limitations under braking in the wet, and allowed wheelspin under acceleration in the wet as well.

Motor Trend was similarly critical of the C41 tyres, noting that they compromised braking distances by their lack of grip. It agreed that the ride could be rough on a rough road, noting that 'high-speed cruising over long distances is tiring.' And it did discover the limits of the swing axles in bends: 'for the owner who likes to drive near his car's limit, we strongly recommend two things: decambering the rear wheels 1–1½ degrees and installing the optional camber compensator.' Having tried both improvements on another, race-prepared Spitfire, the testers had the experience to back up their argument.

The *Motor Trend* report found fault with the seats, which needed more support for the legs and thighs, and felt that the symbols on the instruments were confusing and needed to be learned. (American practice of the time was to label switches with words to describe their function, on the assumption that all users could both read and understand English. Triumph thought that symbols would be more widely understood.) The testers were impressed with the clutch and with how easy the car was to drive and service – the last particularly in view of the accessibility afforded by the forward-hinged front end. They also thought – and probably meant it as a compliment – that the Spitfire 'gives about the most intimate road feel since the Model A Ford.'

Motor Trend had little new to add, but thoroughly enjoyed the car. The tester Danny Collins concluded that he had not had so much fun in a sports car for a long time, but admitted that the fine weather and the stereo tape deck fitted to the test car might have influenced his judgement. That tape deck, incidentally, was a large reel-to-reel machine which took up most of the parcel shelf under the dash on the passenger's side and was definitely not a factory-approved accessory.

Collins found that the Spitfire rode extremely well for a sports car, but he did encounter the swing-axles' oversteer which he tactfully described as 'thrilling to the driver'. He went on, however, to recommend de-cambering the rear wheels if the car were to be used for competitions. As with *Motor Trend*, he found it hard to come to terms with the symbols on the switchgear, and he added a new criticism: that the bumpers were too low down to protect the Spitfire from the bumpers of the average American car.

PRODUCTION CHANGES TO THE SPITFIRE 4

Prototype testing never shows up all the potential problems on a new car, and customer and dealer feedback about the first Spitfires indicated a number of minor areas for improvement. Other modifications were brought about to simplify its manufacturing or assembly. Split-skirt pistons were introduced to replace the original solid-skirt type, and the remote radiator header tank was removed when the cooling

---

What might have been

Triumph was keen to improve the performance of the Spitfire early on, and during 1964 one proposal considered was to replace the 1,147cc engine with an overhead-camshaft Coventry Climax FWE type. This 85bhp engine appears to have been installed in a development car, which achieved a maximum speed of 105mph (168km/h) – well in excess of the production car's 92mph (148km/h) or so. However, the cost of buying in the engine was considered to be too great and so the Mk 2 Spitfire simply had the existing Triumph engine in a higher state of tune.

The twin SU carburettors were on the right of the engine; this is a very early engine with wire gauze AC air filters; later Spitfire 4s had twin paper filters and the Mk 2 engine had a common air-filter box, painted black.

system was found to be too efficient. The original wire-gauze carburettor air filters were replaced by disposable AC paper-element types. In addition, millboard engine side valances, stiffened with steel edging, were added when it became clear that the engine was likely to drown if the car were driven too fast through a deep puddle.

Body modifications began with a reshaped bonnet-closing panel ahead of each A-pillar. The original two-piece, stainless-steel, windscreen trim moulding was replaced by a single-piece plastic type and a shorter stainless-steel finisher was fitted to the rear wing tops when the original was found to hinder the use of one of the hood's

press-studs. The mounting brackets for the rear overriders were redesigned to cure dust leaks into the boot; there were modified door seals; and the original grey floor mats were replaced by black ones.

All these were running changes, however, and of more general interest to Spitfire buyers at the time were the three new options introduced for the car's second season of production. Of these, overdrive was available from October 1963; but for the hardtop and wire wheels customers had to wait until early 1964.

Overdrive was a feature expected of British sports cars, not least because these vehicles traditionally had low gearing to aid acceleration so that their engines would be

A hardtop became available from early in 1964; it was normally finished in the same colour as the body, as seen here.

screaming at high revs during high-speed cruising. The overdrive – effectively a fifth gear which was switched in electrically – lowered the engine revs at cruising speeds and therefore reduced both noise and engine wear. The TR4s had overdrive, and so it was also expected of a Triumph, and no doubt the fact that the rival Austin-Healey Sprite and the MG Midget did not have it must have featured in Triumph's thinking as well. The overdrive chosen was made by Laycock Engineering in Britain, and was their small D-type with 0.82:1 gearing. Once it had

become available by far the majority of new Spitfires were ordered with it.

The hardtop no doubt killed sales of the GRP item with a rather ugly rear window which had been marketed by SAH Accessories since at least the previous autumn. It was made of steel, neatly styled and bolted securely to the windscreen header rail and the rear deck. Cars built from December 1963 had a pair of captive nuts let into the rear deck to aid its fitting.

The third new option was the spoked, knock-off wire wheels, again traditional on

British sports cars and expected for the Spitfire. The ones chosen by Triumph were made by Dunlop and had 60 spokes. They were painted silver rather than chromed, although chrome was used on the eared spinners which locked them to the necessary special splined hubs. Partly to provide additional strength in the wheel (there had been problems with the early wire wheels offered on TR4s), the rim width was increased from the 3.5in of the standard steel wheels to 4.5in – and this no doubt proved an additional incentive to buyers who were concerned about the narrow steel wheels on the Spitfire.

THE SPITFIRE 4 MK 2

The original Spitfire 4 had been such a successful car that not much needed to be

changed. If the money had been available, no doubt Triumph would have looked at improving its swing-axle rear suspension, but the truth was that relatively few owners actually drove their cars hard enough to discover their handling limitations. Those who used their cars for competitions or made a habit of driving near the limit on public roads usually had enough sense to modify the car to tame the waywardness of its back end, so any costly improvement would have been of benefit to only a small number of people who drove beyond the limits of their own capabilites. Consumer protection in the mid-1960s was not what it has since become, and Triumph decided to leave this minority of drivers to reap the rewards of their own stupidity.

However, the car's Spartan interior had been a target of criticism, and so some work was done to improve this. Most obviously,

---

The SAH-tuned Spitfire

Almost as soon as the Spitfire reached the showrooms, amateur and professional mechanics alike began to look at ways of improving its performance. Quickest off the mark seems to have been SAH Accessories of Linslade, near Leighton Buzzard in Bedforshire, who were offering performance conversions for Spitfires by the autumn of 1963. Syd Hurrell's company had been tuning Triumph TR2s and TR3s for many years and had also done some work on the Herald and the Vitesse saloon, and so it was no great surprise to find them turning their hands to the Spitfire as well.

SAH Accessories worked on the 1,147cc engine by enlarging the inlet valves and fitting a high-lift camshaft and twin-choke Solex carburettor. The engine was also balanced and was fitted with Glacier bearings and an oil cooler. Although the power figures for the tuned engine are not available, a test of an SAH-tuned car published in *The Autocar* on 8 November 1963 turned in a maximum speed of 99mph (160km/h) and a 0–60mph (100km/h) time of 13.1 sec as against 92mph (148km/h) and 17.3 sec in the standard car. The magazine noted that the car was very noisy above 3,000rpm, which was partly no doubt a result of its special exhaust manifold.

The tuned SAH engine drove through a competition clutch to wide-rim wheels wearing Dunlop SP radial tyres. The test car also had a modified rear spring (which increased the negative camber of the wheels), competition front springs and adjustable Armstrong dampers all round. An oil-temperature gauge was added to the dashboard and the driver had a lightweight bucket seat on a GRP frame, a wood-rim steering wheel and a matching wooden gear knob. In addition, it carried a GRP hardtop, which was normally supplied unpainted.

'Whilst it could never be described as refined', argued *The Autocar*, 'it was certainly efficient, and several members of the staff felt genuinely nostalgic at its parting when we finally returned it to Leighton Buzzard.'

Spitfire 4 (1962–65) and Spitfire Mk 2 (1965–67)

This picture of a 1965 Mk 2 Show chassis reveals the central backbone chassis frame with its welded outriggers, the simple coil-and-wishbone front suspension and the 1,147cc, four-cylinder engine.

The Mk 2 cars were not easy to distinguish from the original Spitfire 4 at a glance; this 1966 example, however, shows the different grille of the later models: note the absence of vertical bars; the attractive wire wheels were an extra-cost option.

the areas of painted metal visible on the dashboard and the door tops were covered with black leathercloth to give a more luxurious appearance and carpets were standardized in place of the original rubber floor mats. The seats were given more padding and a different pattern of stitching with more white contrast piping, although underneath they used the same frames as before.

From the outside, there was little to distinguish the Mk 2 models from the original Spitfire 4. The quickest way of identifying the newer car was by its new extruded aluminium grille – brighter than the original type and with horizontal bars instead of the honeycomb style. On the boot lid, the chromed script 'Spitfire 4' badge had been joined by a similarly-styled badge reading 'Mk 2'. Small boys keen to distinguish one from another could not even rely on a good memory for the paint colour options, because the first Mk 2s came in exactly the same range of colours as the final Mk 1s.

Other changes were revealed on driving the car, however. The engine now developed

The Mk 2 models brought a different boot lid badging; note the simple 'Mk 2' script added under the original 'Spitfire 4' badge on the right; this car also has the overdrive which was introduced in 1963 and a badge (on the left) to prove it. Note the panoramic rearward view offered by the big window in the optional hardtop.

Triumph Spitfire 4 (1962–64) and Triumph Spitfire 4 Mk 2 (1964–67)

Layout
All-steel bodyshell bolted to steel backbone-frame chassis; two-seater open sports car, with front engine and rear-wheel drive.

Engine

Block material	cast iron
Head material	cast iron
Cylinders	four, in line
Cooling	water
Bore and stroke	69.3mm × 76mm (2.73in × 2.99in)
Capacity	1,147cc (70 cu.in)
Valves	overhead, two per cylinder
Compression ratio	9.0:1
Carburettors	two SU type HS2 (1.25in)
Max. power	63bhp at 5,750rpm (Mk 1 models)
	67bhp at 6,000rpm (Mk 2 models)
Max. torque	67lb.ft at 3,500rpm (Mk 1 models)
	67lb.ft at 3,750rpm (Mk 2 models)

Transmission
Hydraulically-operated Belleville spring washer clutch with 6.25in diameter (diaphragm-spring type with 6.5in diameter from Commission No. FC17136 and on all Mk 2 models); four-speed manual gearbox with synchromesh on 2nd, 3rd and 4th gears only, and optional overdrive (Laycock D-type).

Gearbox ratios

Top	1.00:1
Third	1.39:1
Second	2.16:1
First	3.75:1
Reverse	3.75:1
Overdrive	0.802:1
Final drive ratio 4.11:1	

Suspension and steering

Front	independent, with twin wishbones, coil springs, anti-roll bar and telescopic dampers
Rear	independent. with swing-axles, radius arms, transverse leaf spring and telescopic dampers
Steering	rack and pinion, with 3.75:1 ratio
Tyres	5.20 × 13 crossply; 145 SR 13 radials optional
Wheels	four-stud steel type standard
	centre-lock wire type optional from late 1963
Rim width	3.5in (steel wheels) or 4.5in (wire type)

Brakes

Type	discs at the front
	drums at the rear
Size	disc diameter 9in
	drum diameter 7in, width 1.25in

Dimensions [in(mm)]

Wheelbase	83(2,108)
Track, front	49(1,245)
Track, rear	48(1,220)
Overall length	145(3,680)
Overall width	57(1,450)
Overall height	47.5(1,205)
Unladen weight	1,568lb(711kg)

more power, but at higher crankshaft speeds; and while the maximum torque remained unchanged it was reached at 3,750rpm instead of 3,500. The engine therefore had to be revved harder to give of its best. There was little difference in the low-speed performance, but above about 50mph (80km/h) the Mk 2 Spitfire was noticeably quicker than its predecessor, a fact confirmed by road-test figures in several magazines. The additional power had been achieved by a new camshaft with more overlap and greater lift, together with a tubular extractor-type exhaust manifold which would remain unique to the Mk 2 models. The Mk 2 engine tune was, in fact, the optional Interim tune of the Mk 1 cars, less the Solex carburettor and thus poorer by 3bhp.

The modified engine also addressed a complaint made about the earlier cars that fumes could enter the passenger compartment. To prevent this, it was equipped with a closed-circuit, crankcase breathng system. There was also a sealed cooling system, with an overflow bottle ahead of the radiator. The carburettors now shared a common filter box made of pressed metal, instead of having individual filters, as on the Mk 1 engines, and there was an aluminium cooling fan instead of a steel type. Other changes of note included a diaphragm-spring clutch in place of the Belleville spring-washer type. This shared its 6.5in (165mm) diameter with the later Mk 1 cars and gave a more satisfyingly positive feel to the clutch pedal. For the first time, too, the Commission Number plate of every car carried code numbers identifying the paint and the trim with which it left the Triumph works.

WHAT THE BRITISH PRESS THOUGHT OF THE MK 2

Even though the Mk 2 Spitfire was announced in March 1965, the British press did not rush to road-test the car. Probably the reason was that they thought it was too similar to the old model and that there would therefore be little to write about.

Car and Car Conversions risked a road test, however, and combined it with a report on the the TR4A. They found that EDU 35 C had 'an immense amount of personality' and that, 'like all small sports cars, the Spitfire thrives on a free hand with the gearbox.' The magazine did not like the do-it-yourself soft top, noting that it 'took five minutes and three finger-nails to get on properly'. But it was at pains to defend the Spitfire's handling: 'the Spitfire is one of those very safe cars which needs to be going a darned sight faster than it ever will before anyone with more than a vague idea of how to drive can get into trouble with it.' And, although the swing-axles could be provoked into oversteer, 'whatever happens, there is plenty of warning, and coming unstuck in the Spitfire demands lunacy as a prerequisite.' So much for protests about swing-axle oversteer from the American press, then ...

By the time *Autocar* got round to testing an example of the car in its issue dated 26 August 1966, Triumph's press demonstrator was a wire-wheeled Mk 2 registered as FKV 998 D. Like the staff of *Cars and Car Conversions,* the testers thought that the day of do-it-yourself soft tops was past: 'to match the rest of the equipment, the Spitfire deserves an efficient hood, folding down behind the rear seats, like that fitted to the Herald convertible.'

They complained that the instruments and controls were poorly placed and that the gearbox needed closer ratios; the gap between second and third gear was particu-larly noticeable. The ride was choppy and jolty on rough surfaces, although the body remained pleasingly rigid and rattle-free and the engine tuning had not made the car less tractable in traffic; instead, it had knocked between 1 and 1.5 sec off all the standing-start acceleration times.

Once again, the handling came in for praise, which leads to suspicions that Triumph's public relations people had done their best to counter the reports emanating from across the Atlantic of swing-axle oversteer. The test car car did, of course, have the optional wire wheels with their 4.5in rims and Dunlop SP radial tyres to help, but *Autocar*'s praise was profuse:

> The Spitfire clings to the road better than any Triumph we have driven. On a dry test track at the very giddy (and rapid) limit of adhesion, the tail breaks away in the customary swing-axle fashion, but by then most owners would have backed off, thinking the car would never unstick.

PRODUCTION CHANGES TO THE MK 2 MODELS

As was only to be expected, the Spitfire continued to evolve over the three years of Mk

---

A slant-four Spitfire

Since 1963 Triumph's engine design team under Lewis Dawtrey had been working on a new family of engines. The smaller four-cylinder was designed to be installed with a slant to one side (thus allowing a lower bonnet-line) and was effectively one half of the bigger, V8 engine. A version of the slant-four was sold to Saab for its 1969 99 model and Triumph would later use it in the Dolomite saloon and the TR7. The V8 went on to find a home in the Stag.

Early in 1966 a development slant-four engine was installed in a Spitfire. With 1,709cc and 80bhp, this engine powered the car to 98mph (186km/h). However, this was little better than was available from the 1,296cc engine then in preparation for the Spitfire Mk 3 – and the slant-four engine was not yet ready for production, whereas the 1,296cc type was. As a result the idea was given no further consideration.

2 production. On the mechanical side, the block was bored out to enable the camshaft to run in bearings for the first time and a modified cylinder-head casting brought an improved cooling of the exhaust ports. For the 1966 season, beginning in October 1965, the con-rods were commonized with those of the 1,296cc engine in the new Triumph 1300 front-wheel drive saloon. The crank- shaft rear oil seal was also improved and the sump was equipped with a new drain plug and a modified oil strainer.

The rear dampers were changed and, more visibly, the road wheels were also changed for a similar type with smaller ventilating slots around their rims. The optional door trims with carpeted kick-pads at their leading edges were standardized

---

Triumph tuning kits

In the knowledge that there would be a demand for go-faster Spitfire accessories, and perhaps spurred on by the freelance efforts of SAH Accessories, Triumph prepared three engine-tuning kits which it released on to the market in February 1964. These kits – Interim, Stage I and Stage II – contained engine parts only and other competition items had to be purchased separately. All kits and other competition items were available through Triumph distributors. No one knows how many of each of these kits were actually sold, but it is unlikely that any of them ever found more than a hundred buyers.

The Interim tuning kit took the 63bhp engine up to 70bhp and consisted of a new cylinder head with a 9.75:1 compression ratio, a downdraught Solex 32 PAIA carburettor and a tubular exhaust manifold. The Stage I kit promised 80bhp, although it is doubtful whether any were ever sold. The conversion included a new eight-port cylinder head with a 10.5:1 compression, new inlet and exhaust manifolds and a different camshaft timing. (Whether the original twin SUs were to be replaced by the Solex of the Interim kit has never been clear.) Finally, the Stage II kit took the power up to 90bhp at 6,500rpm by using the eight-port head with a 10.5:1 compression ratio, new inlet and exhaust manifolds, a different camshaft profile and a pair of twin-choke Weber 40DCOE carburettors. The eight-port cylinder head, incidentally, was not the same as the one later used on the Le Mans 'works' racers.

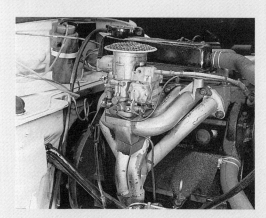

To cater for performance enthusiasts, Triumph introduced a series of bolt-on tuning kits; this is the Interim, or entry-level, kit, with Solex carburettor and tubular exhaust manifold.

The Stage II kit was the best known of the three, because Triumph prepared a demonstrator car (3139 KV) and lent this out to the motoring magazines. *The Motor* published its impressions in the issue of 22 April 1964 and *The Autocar* followed suit in February 1965. *The Autocar* posted a maximum speed of 106mph (170km/h) and 0–60mph (100km/h) in 11.2 sec, noting, however, that the fuel consumption had increased to 23.8mpg (11.9l/100km) from the 31.2mpg (9.1l/100km) of the standard car. 'From a sweet little two-seater tourer', it summarized, 'it becomes a sporty little ball of fire with performance extremely close to that of its big brother the TR4.'

Factory-installed options

Brake master cylinder extension
Carpets (Vitesse-type material) (standard on Mk 2 cars)
Competition rear spring
Door trim with carpeted kick pad (standard from FC 56578)
Hardtop (introduced in early 1964)
Ignition coil giving 7-volt cold start
Laminated windscreen
Leather upholstery (black, blue or red)
Overdrive (introduced in early 1964)
Skid plate
Starter solenoid for cold start
Steering-column lock
Tail-light fuse
Tonneau cover (black or white, to match soft top)

Dealer accessories: Spitfire 4

Badge bar
Bonnet lock
Boot rack for luggage
Cigarette lighter
Continental touring kit
Defroster
Engine bay valances (cars before FC 20753)
Fog lamp (4in, 50W Eversure sealed-beam type)
Fuel filter
Heater
Hub-cap removal tool
Locking petrol cap
Radio (Smith's Radiomobile) and wing aerial
Reversing lamp
Rocker cover with chrome plating
Seat belts (two-point fixing)
Spot lamp (4in, 50W Eversure sealed-beam type)
Sun visors
Touch-in paints (available as pencil or spray can)
Tow bar (by Witter)
Wheel-trim ring (Vitesse-type)
Whitewall tyres (4-ply rating)
Wing mirror (Magnatex D-type)
Wire wheels (from early 1964 only)

In addition, approved tuning kits were available through Triumph dealers; see separate box.

The Spitfire soon began to acquire a reputation in competition; this early example was posed with Stirling Moss and his protégée Val Pirie, early in 1964.

and the lever-type exterior door handles were changed for fixed handles with a press-button release. The keylock was no longer incorporated in the handle itself from this point, but was located separately underneath it. At the same time, a keylock was fitted to the passenger door for the first time and anti-burst latches were installed.

CONTEMPORARIES AND RIVALS

It is worth putting the Spitfire into context by noting that its price in the basic trim

(£530 in Britain in 1962, rising to £550 by 1966) was about one-third that of a Jaguar E-type and matched roughly that of a mundane family saloon in the 1,200–1,500cc class. The E-type had been introduced in 1961 and was the sensation of the time. In May 1962 – a few months ahead of the Spitfire – Triumph introduced its Vitesse, which was a six-cylinder edition of the Herald and would ultimately lead on to the GT6 model based on the Spitfire. In 1963 Triumph announced its new 2000 saloon, at exactly the same time as the rival Rover 2000; and at the time when the Spitfire Mk 2 was introduced in 1965, Rolls-Royce

---

Dealer accessories: Spitfire 4 Mk 2

The items listed below were available in addition to those offered for the Mk 1 cars and listed elsewhere. They should not be considered exclusive to the Mk 2 cars, however, as in most cases it was possible to fit them to earlier, Mk 1, models.

Anti-mist panel for hardtop
Brake servo (Girling Powerstop)
Competition brake pads (Ferodo DS 11)
Competition front springs
Competition rear springs
Competition ignition coil (Lucas HA 12)
Competition rev counter (to 8,000rpm)
Fire extinguisher
Hood sealer (black or clear)
Hub-cap medallion
Mud flaps (rear only)
Oil cooler
Radial tyres (Dunlop SP41 145x13 or 155x13)
Rear hub bearing and sealing kit
Seat belts, three-point type (the two-point type was then still available)
Seat covers (by Karobes)
Sill protector panel (black plastic)
Ski-rack attachment for boot rack
Soft top (for cars supplied with a hardtop when new)
Tailpipe finisher in chrome
Trunnion sealing kit
Underseal (by Carseal)
Wide-rim wheels (4.5in rim)
Wing mirrors: six different types (by Magnetron, Morgan and Wingard)
Wood-rim steering wheel

---

announced its first monocoque cars with the names of the Silver Shadow and Bentley T-type.

These were interesting times for the British motor industry too, for they witnessed the beginnings of the roller-coaster of takeovers and mergers which ended with the formation of British Leyland in 1968. Standard-Triumph was, in fact, the first big company to go, when it was bought by Leyland Motors in 1961. Jaguar meanwhile had acquired Daimler, and then Rover bought Alvis in 1965. BMC went on to buy Pressed Steel, and this acquisition caused Rover to panic and join the Leyland Motors

fold in 1967. Jaguar formed an alliance with BMC as British Motor Holdings, and by the time the Spitfire Mk 2 was replaced by the Mk 3 model in 1967, the British government was already plotting to bring BMH and Leyland together to make a company big enough to face up to the powerful European and American combines.

For most of the period of their availability, the Spitfire 4 and the Spitfire 4 Mk 2 were competing for sales with the same group of small sports cars. These were the Austin-Healey Sprite and its slightly more expensive MG Midget twin and, in the bespoke market, the Morgan 4/4. The BMC

Identification and production: Spitfire 4 and Spitfire 4 Mk 2

The Commission Number of a Spitfire will be found on a plate rivetted to the left-hand door pillar. This number is the same as what other manufacturers call the chassis number and what is nowadays usually called a VIN or Vehicle Identification Number. The sequences for Spitfire 4 and Spitfire 4 Mk 2 cars are as follows:

Spitfire 4	FC1 to FC 44656
Spitfire 4 Mk 2	FC50001 to FC88904

In theory, therefore, there were 44,656 Mk 1 cars and 38,904 Mk 2s. However, these totals are at variance with the production figures given in other Triumph records, where it appears that 45,754 Mk 1s and 37,408 Mk 2s were built. Unfortunately, even the totals do not agree: the chassis numbers give 83,560 while the production totals amount to 83,162. The contradictions remain unresolved at present, despite the best efforts of Anders Clausager at the British Motor Industry Heritage Trust, whose calculations have produced the figures used here.

The engine numbers for these cars fall within the same sequences as the Commission Numbers (although the serial numbers should not be expected to match). Spitfire Mk 1 engines have numbers below FC50000 and Spitfire Mk 2 engines have numbers from FC50001. Gearboxes and differentials also have FC prefixes to their serial numbers.

---

twins were both cheaper than the Spitfire, although that must surely have been the main reason for buying one in preference to the Triumph because they were neither as good looking nor as well-equipped as the Canley-built car. In the USA, however, perhaps the prominence given in press reports to the Triumph's swing-axle oversteer *in extremis* might have persuaded some buyers that the BMC cars were a safer bet ...

As for the Morgan 4/4, its appeal was really rather different from that of the Spitfire. The Morgan was an old-school sports car, with styling to match and a rock-hard ride, and it was most certainly not available straight off the showroom floor because each car was built to an individual order. From 1966 Honda entered the small sports-car market with its S800, but in Britain its inflated price (over £632 before purchase tax, when a Spitfire was £550 and a Mk IV Sprite £545) put off most buyers. For real motoring entertainment, however, albeit without the soft top which must have been the deciding factor for many motorists, the Morris Mini-Cooper was hard to beat at a price much lower than the Spitfire's.

Performance figures, Spitfire 4 and Spitfire 4 Mk 2

Both the Spitfire 4 and the Spitfire 4 Mk 2 had maximum speeds of around 92mph (147km/h). This speed was achieved on direct top gear and was not normally achievable in overdrive. The Mk 2 model was quicker through the gears, however, reaching 60mph from rest in about 15.5 sec, some 2 sec before the earlier car. Fuel consumption for both types was normally between 33 and 35mpg (8.6 and 8.1l/100km); better consumption was achievable with a light foot.

Paint and trim colours, Spitfire 4

October 1962 – May 1963
There were seven exterior colours and three interior colours; the combinations available were as follows:

Body colour	Upholstery colour
Black	black, blue or red
Lichfield Green	black or red
Pale Yellow	black
Phantom Grey	red
Powder Blue	black or blue
Signal Red	black or red
Spa White	black, blue or red

June 1963 – July 1964
The range was reduced to six, of which only two (Black and Signal Red) were carried over from the previous season; black and red interior trims remained, but the third was now called midnight blue; the options were:

Body colour	Upholstery colour
Black	red
Conifer Green	black
Jonquil Yellow	black
Signal Red	black
Wedgwood Blue	Midnight Blue
White	black or red

August – September 1964
The range was temporarily reduced to five with the loss of Jonquil Yellow; the other colours and combinations remained unchanged.

October – November 1964
The range increased to six again for the last two month of Spitfire 4 (Mk 1) production, with the addition of one new colour; the five earlier ones and the trim combinations remained unchanged; the new choices were:

Body colour	Upholstery colour
Royal Blue	black or Midnight Blue

Paint and trim colours, Spitfire 4 Mk 2

All Mk 2 Spitfires had the code numbers of their original body and trim colours stamped on to their chassis number plates. Where known, these code numbers are given in brackets in the lists which follow. In some cases the same code number was used for both the body colour and the trim colour.

December 1964 – September 1965
There were six exterior and three interior colours; the combinations available were the same as on the final Mk 1 cars and were as follows:

Body colour	*Upholstery colour*
Black (11)	red
Conifer Green (25)	black
Royal Blue (56)	black or Midnight Blue
Signal Red (32)	black
Wedgwood Blue (26)	Midnight Blue
White (19)	black or red

October 1965 – January 1967
Black was dropped from the range, leaving the remaining five exterior and the three interior colours as before, with the same availability of combinations.

3 GT6: Development and Mk 1 Models (1966–68)

By the middle of 1963 the Spitfire had been successfully launched and the once-ailing Standard-Triumph company was rapidly returning to financial health. So engineering director Harry Webster began to look to the future with rather more confidence than had been possible when the original Bomb prototype had been delivered to Canley from Michelotti's studios in Turin. The Triumph 2000 saloon was launched in the autumn to replace the Standard Vanguard Six and work began on the car which would become the TR4A at the beginning of 1965, as well as on a new front-wheel drive small saloon which was intended to replace the Herald.

Yet even with this big workload on his relatively small engineering department, Webster also found time to look at the Spitfire. The minor but worthwhile improvements which turned the car into a Mk 2 model in 1965 have been examined in Chapter 2, but these were far from being Webster's only ideas. Much more far-reaching was the plan to develop a GT version of the Spitfire, by which he meant a derivative with a fastback coupé body. This would have the same relationship to the open Spitfire as the Jaguar E-type coupé had to the convertible model; in other words, it would have a proper steel-roofed bodyshell rather than a simple, detachable hardtop. He raised the issue at the Triumph board meeting in August 1963 and again at the board's December meeting. On this second occasion, a launch date of October 1964 was mooted, but no firm decisions were taken.

Never one to waste time – nor to waste unnecessary time waiting for board approval – Webster had already asked Michelotti to sketch a fastback body for the Spitfire, using as many existing panels as possible. Michelotti responded with his usual speed, and car number X691, the first of the two British-built prototypes completed in 1962, was shipped back to Turin to be converted into the chosen style. Triumph invariably extracted the maximum use from their prototype cars. While X691 (4305 VC) was being converted into the prototype Spitfire GT in Turin, its sister car X692 (412 VC) was being prepared as a rally car to give Triumph some idea of how to equip the rally Spitfires which were being planned for 1964. Several years later Michelotti would also convert the prototype Stag from an open car to a closed fastback coupé, although that project never came to fruition. In the case of the Spitfire GT it most certainly did.

The prototype Spitfire GT had an elegantly sloping roof and a top-hinged tailgate. Below that it retained the standard Spitfire body, although the fuel tank had been relocated in order to give an unobstructed space behind the seats and under the big tailgate. There was also a new dashboard, with the major dials directly ahead of the driver and the auxiliary gauges in a row in the centre. The result was a most attractive car, finished in bright

The GT6 started life as a 'Spitfire GT', modified from Spitfire prototype X691 by Michelotti; Triumph liked the fastback shape but did not adopt Michelotti's restyled dashboard, seen here. When this picture was taken in November 1963 the car still had its original four-cylinder engine.

red, which nevertheless proved a little disappointing when it went out on the road. The problem was that the extra metal of the fastback roof added weight, and that slowed the car down. It was quite obvious that the buying public were not going to pay a premium for a Spitfire GT which was slower than the open car, and it was equally obvious that the coupé would cost more to build than the open car.

Undaunted, Webster decided to have the prototype fitted with the small six-cylinder engine which had been introduced in the Vitesse during 1962. The main problems of installing this in the space originally designed to accommodate a four-cylinder engine had already been solved because the Vitesse had been developed from the Herald. In addition, the twin-carburettor, 1,588cc engine's 77bhp would offer both better performance and more refinement than the 63bhp 1,147cc engine in the standard Spitfire. Thus in the early months of 1964 X691 was equipped with a Vitesse engine, but retained its standard Spitfire gearing of 4.11:1 overall.

There was only one major modification necessary, and that was to the bonnet panel. The six-cylinder engine was rather longer than the four-cylinder and, while it fitted comfortably under the bonnet of the Herald saloon to make the Vitesse, it would not fit so comfortably under the sloping nose of the Spitfire. Therefore the bonnet panel of X691 was given a rough-and-ready bulge to make room, with an open air intake at the forward end. The results were promising, but still not good enough. The Spitfire GT with its six-cylinder engine was still not convincingly faster than the existing production car and was only barely capable of 100mph (160km/h).

The solution to the dilemma more or less presented itself. The performance of the 1,588cc engine had disappointed American customers for the Vitesse (where the car was sold as a Triumph Sports Six) and it was going to be necessary to increase the power of this car as well. The obvious way of doing this was to use the 1,998cc engine already in production for the 2000 saloon. It was a big-bore cousin of the 1,588cc type, and would fit into the Vitesse's engine bay without any difficulty. If it could be made to

fit the Vitesse, it could be made to fit the Spitfire GT as well, thus simplifying the engineering development needed to create two new models and retaining the commonality between models which is so desirable in both assembly and servicing. Another factor also came into play at about this time. This was that MG was known to be planning a fastback coupé or GT derivative of the MGB sports car. With a 2-litre engine, the six-cylinder Spitfire GT could make a credible competitor for that car, which would otherwise steal sales in an area where Triumph was not represented.

Following the practice established with the Spitfire, where the original rolling-concept car had been followed by two prototypes, Triumph now built a pair of fastback coupés with the 2-litre engine. Both also had the stronger final drive unit which was to be shared with the 2-litre Vitesse, and the all-synchromesh gearbox which had been pioneered on the works racing and rally Spitfires. Car number X742 had right-hand drive and was completed in April 1965; the dates suggest that it was built alongside the prototype Mk 3 Spitfire, which was numbered X743 and registered as EVC 376C. Car number X746 had left-hand drive and was registered on

The GT6 and the works Spitfires

Enthusiasts have often wondered about the connection between the GT6 styling and the fastback bodies used on the Spitfires which the Triumph Competitions Department fielded during 1964–65. Were the competition cars' glass-fibre tops the inspiration for the GT6 and how did they fit into the chronology of GT6 development?

The answer is disarmingly simple: by the time the Engineering Department had started work on the four Le Mans cars which were the first to carry the fastback bodies, Michelotti had already delivered his fastback prototype to Canley. It looked good enough and it was ready to hand – so a mould was taken from it and the competition cars' glass-fibre roofs were made from that. The shape proved successful enough for Triumph to use it on the rally Spitfires as well later (see Chapter 7), and it appears that no wind-tunnel or other aerodynamic testing was ever carried out. If it worked on the competition cars, ran the reasoning, it will work all right in production, too.

This left-hand drive, prototype 'Spitfire GT' was built in 1965 and had the experimental commission number X746; the six-cylinder, 2-litre engine fitted neatly into the space available.

25 November 1965. They carried the number plates EVC 375C and FWK 319D, respectively, and incorporated a number of modifications which experience with the original Spitfire GT had suggested.

The lashed-up air intake on the modified bonnet of X691 gave way to a more streamlined and rounded bonnet bulge, and louvres were let into the bonnet top towards the back on each side to maintain an adequate flow of cooling air. Meanwhile, cockpit ventilation had also proved to be a problem and therefore the new cars were fitted with swivelling front quarter-win-

dows and their rear side windows were hinged at the front to give a flow of air right through the passenger compartment. By this time the car had lost its Spitfire name and was known within Triumph as the GT6, a name which would be retained for production. And, although the GT6 was most certainly a derivative of the Spitfire and would always be related to it in a large number of ways, the dropping of the Spitfire name certainly allowed the marketing people to promote the car as a different and more up-market model.

Development work continued through

1965 and into 1966, but by the summer of that year the design was thought to be good enough for release. It was thus given over to the production department, which arranged that Pressed Steel should provide the new fastback roof panels and that these should be assembled to modified Spitfire shells at the Forward Radiator plant in Bordesley Green. The first of the new GT6 models started coming off the assembly lines at Canley in July 1966, in preparation for a public launch that October.

THE GT6 ON SALE

There was never any doubt that the GT6 was developed primarily for the North American market. Even though it was announced for the rest of the world at the Paris Motor Show in October 1966, customers outside the USA had to wait until full production was achieved in January 1967 before they had any chance of getting their hands on a car. Every example of the GT6 made before then was sent to the USA.

The production specification of the GT6 had finally been settled in the first half of 1966, and the car was equipped with a 95bhp version of the 2-litre engine which gave it a maximum speed of around 106mph (170km/h) and a 0–60mph (100km/h) acceleration of about 12 sec. There may be more than mere coincidence in that the engine's output was exactly the same as that of the contemporary MGB GT, of course... The four-speed close-ratio gearbox had synchromesh on all gears, and was coupled to a tall 3.27:1 final drive or to a 3.89:1 unit when overdrive was fitted. There were bigger discs and calipers than on the Spitfire and the rear drums were larger, too, with an 8in (203mm) diameter. Wheels had 4.5in rims, whether they were the standard disc type or the optional centre-lock wires, and 155 × 13 radial tyres were standard wear. Steering was again a responsive rack-and-pinion system, but with lower gearing to compensate for the extra weight of the six-cylinder engine.

Like the Spitfire, the GT6 was a two-seater, and the whole of the floor area beneath its big tailgate was covered with carpet so that luggage could be stowed

The GT6 prototypes

Number	Registration	Build date	Engine	Remarks
X 691	4305 VC	1963	initially 4-cyl 1,147cc, later 6-cyl 1,588cc; finally	built in 1962 as a Spitfire prototype; sent to Michelotti in Turin during late 1963 for conversion to fast back
			no. HE 18491 HE	coupé; eventually used for fuel injection and exhaust emissions work
X 742	EVC 375 C	April 1965	1,998cc, no. X 1042 E	right-hand drive, used for 4,000-mile endurance
X 746	FWK 319 D	24 Nov 1965	1,998cc	test left-hand drive, fitted with 'safety facia'; later equipped with fuel injection and lent to Lucas Industries

The Triumph six-cylinder engine

Triumph's 2-litre engine began life during the late 1950s at the time when the company was planning a replacement saloon for the Standard Vanguard and the Ensign model. Board approval for work to start on the new car, which carried the project name Zebu, was given in August 1957 and it was originally planned to enter production during 1960. The company started work on a new overhead-valve, six-cylinder engine which was intended specifically for the car and was expected to have two capacities. There would be a 1.5-litre type (for the model to replace the Standard Ensign) and a 2-litre type (to replace the Vanguard). This engine was based on the design of the existing four-cylinder.

Both engines shared their 76mm stroke with the four-cylinder, overhead-valve Standard engine which could trace its ancestry back to the early 1950s and would go on to power the Herald, and the 2-litre version even shared its 74.7mm bore with the 1,147cc version of that engine. Both were also ready on schedule, but in the meantime the timing of the Zebu project had slipped when it ran into styling difficulties. The Vanguard range was already in decline, so the new 2-litre engine was swiftly dropped into the engine bay formerly occupied by the slightly larger-capacity, four-cylinder engine, and for 1961 Standard introduced the Vanguard Six. It was, admittedly, a holding operation, but it did allow the company to gain valuable experiece of the new engine in service.

By July 1961 the Zebu project had been scrapped and Triumph were working on a new car with the codename Barb. This one, with styling by Michelotti, was the car which became the Triumph 2000 and was eventually launched in 1963. However, in the beginning there were plans for a Barb derivative to replace the Standard Ensign, the 'cheap' version of the Vanguard, and to that end some prototypes ran with the smaller version of the six-cylinder engine, which by now displaced 1,596cc.

However, these plans changed during 1962. The proposed Triumph 1600 was dropped as a project, mainly to allow the new 2000 to compete on more equal terms with Rover's planned new 2000; to have a smaller-engined, cheaper version on sale as well was considered not to be good marketing policy. Thus the 1,596cc engine ended up being used to turn the Herald into a Vitesse in 1962.

Later, that 1,596cc engine would go into a Spitfire GT prototype, would give a disappointing performance and would be replaced in both this car and the Vitesse by the 2-litre engine.

The Triumph six-cylinder engine was later developed even further, into a long-stroke, 2.5-litre version. There were fuel-injected versions of this in its final guise and the engine served as the basis of the further-developed overhead-camshaft Triumph engines which appeared in the Rover 2300 and the 2600 saloon between 1977 and 1986. The engine was available in other Standard-Triumph products as follows:

1,596cc ('1600') engine   66.75mm bore × 76mm stroke
Vitesse 1600, 1962–66:   two Solex, 8.75:1 compression, 70bhp at 5,000rpm and 92lb.ft at 2,800rpm
1,998cc ('2-litre') engine   74.7mm bore × 66mm stroke
Vanguard Six, 1961–63   two Solex, 8.0:1 compression, 80bhp at 4,500rpm and
2000 Mk 1, 1963–69   two Zenith-Stromberg, 8.5:1 compression, 90bhp at 5,000rpm and 117lb.ft at 2,900rpm
Vitesse 2-litre, 1966–68   two Zenith-Stromberg, 9.5:1 compression, 95bhp at 5,000rpm and 117lb.ft at 3,000rpm
Vitesse 2-litre, 1968–71   two Zenith-Stromberg, 9.25:1 compression, 104bhp at 5,300rpm and 117lb.ft at 3,000rpm

The Triumph six-cylinder engine *(continued)*	
2000 Mk 2, 1969–73	two Zenith-Stromberg, 9.25:1 compression, 84bhp at 5,000rpm and 100lb.ft at 2,900rpm *
2000 Mk 2, 1973–75	two Zenith-Stromberg, 8.8:1 compression, 84bhp at 5,000rpm and 100lb.ft at 2,900rpm*
2000TC, 1975–77	two SU 8.8:1 compression, 91bhp at 4,750rpm and 110lb.ft at 3,300rpm*
2,498cc ('2.5-litre') engine	74.7mm bore × 95mm stroke
TR5, 1967–68	Lucas injection, 9.5:1 compression, 150bhp at 5,500rpm and 164lb.ft at 3,500rpm
TR250, 1967–68	two Strombergs, 8.5:1 compression, 104bhp at 4,500rpm and 143lb.ft at 3,000rpm
TR6, 1969–72	as TR5
TR6, 1973–75	Lucas injection, 9.5:1 compression, 124bhp at 5,000rpm and 143lb.ft at 3,500rpm*
TR6 (Federal), 1969–76	as TR250
2.5PI Mk 1, 1968–69	Lucas injection, 9.5:1 compression, 132bhp at 5,500rpm and 153lb.ft at 2,000rpm
2.5PI Mk 2, 1969–75	as 2.5PI Mk 1
2500TC, 1974–75	two SU 8.5:1 compression, 99bhp at 4,700rpm and 133lb.ft at 3,000rpm*
2500TC, 1975–77	two SU 8.5:1 compression, 106bhp at 4,700rpm and 139lb.ft at 3,000rpm*
2500S, 1975–77	as 2500TC

Note: all figures are to SAE nett standards except those marked with an asterisk (*) which are to DIN standards.

The original GT6 had clean lines which were somehow lost on the Mk 2 models; this early example shows off the low-mounted bumpers (as on the contemporary Spitfire Mk 2), the Vitesse-style wheel-trim rings and the absence of louvres from the fastback. The earliest examples of the GT6 were for export only and Triumph emphasized the fact by releasing pictures of a left-hand drive car, FKV 83D, when production began.

The sleek lines of the fastback and the bonnet louvres are seen in this picture of an early car, equipped with the optional wire wheels.

This well-preserved, late example was brought along to the Triumph 75th Anniversary celebration at Gaydon in summer 1998.

The large filler cap on the left-hand side of the rear panel helped to emphasize the car's sporting heritage and was a reminder that the fuel tank had been relocated from its Spitfire position; it is just possible to see that the rear quarter-windows are open here.

Tail lamps, indicators, reversing lamps and bumpers were all identical to their Spitfire counterparts.

there. Under the front edge of the load platform was a cubby hole for concealing small items. Unlike the Mk 2 Spitfire of the day, there was full carpeting in the footwells and there was also a much more luxurious dashboard with a polished walnut finish. More important, it carried the speedometer and rev counter directly in front of the driver rather than in the centre where they were sometimes hard to see. Switchgear and controls were taken from the 1300

saloon, and there was a leather-rimmed steering wheel with a smaller (15in; 380mm) diameter than the one in the Spitfire. The seats were a new design based on rally-type seats, and between them there was even a padded armrest.

These features helped to create a very different character for the GT6. It was not just a Spitfire with a solid roof and a more powerful engine, but an altogether more refined grand touring car. Performance was

Triumph GT6 (1966–68)

Layout
All-steel bodyshell bolted to steel backbone-frame chassis; two-seater fastback coupé, with front engine and rear-wheel drive.

Engine

Block material	cast iron
Head material	cast iron
Cylinders	six, in line
Cooling	water
Bore and stroke	74.7mm × 76mm (2.94in × 2.99in)
Capacity	1,998cc (122 cu.in)
Valves	overhead, two per cylinder
Compression ratio	9.0:1
Carburettors	two Zenith-Stromberg type 150 CD
Max. power	95bhp at 5,000rpm
Max. torque	117.3lb.ft at 3,000rpm

Transmission
Hydraulically-operated diaphragm clutch with 8.5in diameter; four-speed, all-synchromesh manual gearbox with optional overdrive (Laycock D-type).

Gearbox ratios

Top	1.00:1
Third	1.25:1
Second	1.78:1
First	2.65:1
Reverse	3.10:1
Overdrive	0.802:1
Final drive ratio	3.27:1 (non-overdrive) or 3.89:1 (overdrive)

Suspension and steering

Front	independent, with twin wishbones, coil springs, anti-roll bar and telescopic dampers
Rear	independent, with swing-axles, radius arms, transverse leaf spring and telescopic dampers
Steering	rack and pinion, with 4.3:1 ratio
Tyres	155 SR 13 radial
Wheels	four-stud steel type standard
	centre-lock wire type optional (standard in USA)
Rim width	4.5in

Brakes

Type	discs at the front
	drums at the rear
Size	disc diameter 9.7in
	drum diameter 8in, width 1.25in

Dimensions [in(mm)]	
Wheelbase	83(2,108)
Track, front	49(1,245)
Track, rear	48in(1,220)
Overall length	145(3,680)
Overall width	57(1,450)
Overall height	47(1,195)
Unladen weight	1,904lb(865kg)

irreproachable, but the GT6 was not a sports car. Its suspension, while using the same basic hardware as the Spitfire, was tuned for a softer ride and the whole car gave the impression that it was set up for driving long distances at high speed. The Spitfire, by contrast, always felt more of a point-and-squirt machine.

All this made it doubly surprising that the overdrive and the heater were still options costing more money on the GT6. Both really belonged in the basic specification of the car, but it seems probable that Triumph had left them out as a way of bringing the cost of the GT6 down to a long way below that of the MGB GT which had been introduced a year earlier. Adding both

to the car certainly did put its cost up above that of its rival from Abingdon.

WHAT THE BRITISH PRESS SAID

The first full test of the new GT6 was published in *Motor* on 29 October 1966, although the magazine's staff had managed a brief drive in a car a fortnight earlier and had then published some favourable first impressions. The fuller test praised the 'serene ferocity' of the car's acceleration, although it was noted that the engine did not feel very sporting despite plenty of low-speed punch. First gear was a

The GT6 proudly displayed the old Standard-Triumph badge just ahead of its bonnet bulge; its chromed grille was also used on the Spitfire Mk 3, where the raised bumper nevertheless tended to hide it from view.

Factory-installed options: GT6 Mk 1

Alternator (11ACR type)
Competition brake linings
Grease nipples for front upper ball joints
Grease nipples for track rod ends
Heater
Laminated windscreen
Leather upholstery and trim
Overdrive
Skid plate
Steering-column lock

---

little stiff to use; there was whine in the lower gears; and the overdrive engaged and disengaged with a jerk.

The handling and brakes were good enough to enable the performance to be used to the full in safety, although the steering was rather dead-feeling and, almost inevitably, 'one vice mars the excellence of roadholding and handling'. This was, of course, lift-off oversteer. Other criticisms focused on the ventilation of the passenger compartment, the confusing column switches, and the fact that a 6ft (1.83m) driver could only just get comfortable behind the wheel.

Car magazine also ran a road test report on the GT6 in its October 1966 issue. The testers thought that the car felt entirely different from a Spitfire, being more solid and substantial. Generally speaking, their views were favourable, but they did note that the car's propensity to tail slides meant that it had to be treated with some respect. They also thought that buyers were entitled to better detailed design at this price and singled out the cluttered tail with its profusion of lamps and badges as a weakness. They commented that the car also deserved more model identification than it carried.

When *Autocar* finally tested a GT6 it was

nearly a year later, in its issue dated 7 September 1967. The test team were divided in their opinions, some members considering that the limitations of the swing-axle rear suspension and the poor ventilation were enough to spoil the car, while others thought that these were forgivable failings. But failings they were, and the report was particularly scathing about the lift-off oversteer and the bottoming of the rear suspension on rough roads: 'It is a pity that the limitations from the continued use of swing axles should detract so much from what is basically such a good car, and we urge Standard-Triumph to make improvements without delay.'

The testers also found that the low-geared steering was too imprecise to allow the car to be driven tidily at speed. They shared the views expressed in earlier tests that the interior was cramped, that the ventilation was poor and that the overdrive was jerky in operation. 'Potentially', they concluded, 'the GT6 is a fine formula; with further development (and if necessary a price increase) it could become outstanding.'

The last of the major magazines to run a test on the Mk 1 GT6 was *Car*. Having already reported on the model a year earlier, the magazine now ran a comparison test

Dealer accessories: GT6 Mk 1

Anti-frost shield for windscreen
Auxiliary gauge mounting panel for one instrument
Auxiliary gauge mounting panel for two instruments
Bonnet lock
Brake servo (Girling Power Stop type)
Cigarette lighter (on bracket)
Continental touring kit
Electric windscreen defroster
Emergency windscreen
Fire extinguisher
Fog lamp (Styla quartz–iodine type)
Fuel-tank filter
Head-rest
Heated rear window
Hub-cap medallion
Luggage straps (pair, leather)
Mudflaps (rear wheels only)
Oil cooler (from KC5001 only)
Paints (touch-in)
Radio (Smith's Radiomobile) and aerial
Roof rack
Safety belts (two-point fixing to KC1040; three-point thereafter)
Safety-warning triangle
Sill protectors
Spark-plug spanner (Plugmaster type)
Spot lamp (Styla quartz–iodine type)
Steering-wheel glove (brown leather)
Steering-wheel glove (brown simulated leather)
Tow bar
Tow rope and luggage-rack strap
Wing mirrors
Wire wheels (supplied with eared spinners up to KC7875 and with hexagonal spinners thereafter)
Wheelbrace (Lever Master type)
Wood-rim steering wheel

Among the wide variety of exterior mirrors available for the GT6 was this 'racing' type, which fitted to the door. Note the rubber seal at the base of the windscreen frame; even though the screen and its frame were not removable from these cars, they were nevertheless the same components as on the Spitfire.

between the GT6 and an MGB GT. This was an obvious comparison to make, but in many ways was quite revealing. The MG had the advantage of token rear seats which made it more versatile, while Triumph did not even pretend that there might be room for children in the back of the GT6. The test team considered that neither car really lived up to the promise of the GT title because both offered insufficient comfort and neither was really fast enough. However, the MG took their

The badging of the first GT6s is displayed to good effect on this Belgian-registered example, which nevertheless has right-hand drive.

collective vote in the end. They thought it was better looking, offered more shoulder room and was both quieter and better handling. These were qualities for which they would be prepared to sacrifice the Triumph's slightly better performance.

THE GT6 IN THE USA

As the GT6 had been designed primarily for the USA, there was almost nothing special about the North American versions of the car during the Mk 1 production run. However, all of them did have centre-lock wire wheels as standard and special brackets for mounting US-style number plates. Narrow-band, whitewall tyres appear to have been standard wear (and Goodyear G800s were supplied as alternatives to the Dunlop SP41s also seen in Britain), and the 1968 models also had a limited amount of emissions-control equipment on their engines.

WHAT THE AMERICAN PRESS SAID

Road and Track had more to say about the GT6 than any other American magazine,

---

Identification and production: GT6 Mk 1

The Commission Number of a GT6 is on a plate rivetted to the left-hand door pillar. The sequence for these models was: KC1 to KC13752. In theory, therefore, there were 13,752 Mk 1 cars. However, the production figures given in other Triumph records suggest that 15,818 cars were actually built, a number which will not comfortably fit between the two extremes of the known Commission Number sequence. The contradiction remains unresolved at present.

The engine numbers for these cars fall within the same sequences as the Commission Numbers (although the serial numbers should not be expected to match). Engines, gearboxes and differentials all have KC prefixes to their serial numbers, except that 1968-model emissions-controlled engines for the American market have numbers beginning with KD 5001.

Going faster: the SAH-tuned GT6

Triumph never offered many competition accessories for the GT6, probably because they viewed it more as a refined grand tourer than as a weekend racer such as the Spitfire. This left the market wide open for Triumph tuners SAH of Linslade, who turned their attention to the GT6 in the same way as they had to other models from Canley. From the autumn of 1967 they offered five stages of engine tuning, together with a variety of additional accessories to improve the handling or simply to improve the appearance of the car.

Handling improvements were effected by using Minilite spoked alloy wheels with 5.5in rims at the rear and 5in rims at the front, in each case with Pirelli Cinturato 165x13 tyres. The rear wheels also had a different offset from the fronts, which widened the rear track. By February 1968 the company offered a Le Mans fibreglass bonnet assembly, which saved around 40lb (18kg) in weight as compared with the standard steel type, and also provided faired-in lamps and side louvres in a style similar to those of the works Le Mans Spitfire racers.

The five stages of engine tune were:

Stage 1	Modified cylinder head, with SAH '26' camshaft, six-branch exhaust manifold and carburation changes; this added about 26bhp to the engine's output.
Stage 2	Reworked cylinder head with larger inlet valves, balanced and polished combustion chambers and ports, and a 10.5:1 compression ratio, plus other modifications as Stage 1.
Stage 3	As Stage 2, but with Tecalemit-Jackson fuel injection; this added about 50bhp to the engine's output.
Stage 4	As Stage 2, but with three Weber carburettors and SAH '47' camshaft.
Stage 5	As Stage 3, but with the SAH '47' camshaft.

The '26' camshaft gave timings of 26,63, 63 and 26 degrees, while the '47' camshaft gave timings of 40,70,70 and 40 degrees. An oil cooler was standard from Stage 3 upwards.

In 1967–68 a number of British magazines tested the SAH demonstrator car. The maximum speed with the Stage 4 and the Stage 5 conversion was estimated at 120–125mph (193–200km/h), and the Stage 4 conversion gave a 0–60mph time of 8.4 sec when tested by *Motor* in the issue dated 28 October 1967.

following a first report in November 1966 with a more detailed appraisal in January 1968. The earlier report noted that the car 'does not feel as fast as it is', and was cautiously optimistic about the handling: 'the Triumph engineers... reckon that the extra front end weight makes this GT Six behave more gently than a Spitfire 4 when pushed to breakaway.'

The later report was rather more realistic about the swing-axle suspension, advising that 'one should plan cornering maneuvers well in advance, and stick to the plan.' The magazine complained of poor ventilation, a lack of room in the cockpit for anyone over 5ft 8in (1.74m) tall or with hips bigger than 40in (103cm), and that the rear suspension would bottom on rough surfaces. However, 'on straight acceleration,the GT6 is a joy'.

In January 1967 *Sports Car Graphic* published its impressions of the car, gained in Britain by an English journalist. The GT6 was described as 'well-furnished and fully equipped', although interior ventilation again came in for criticism. Effortless cruising in the 80–90mph (125–145km/h) range was possible, but the SP41 radials held the car in place well and, at Mallory Park racing circuit on the press launch, the car impressed: 'Believe me, this car handles!' It was a disappointment to find the swing-axles still in evidence, but 'the additional total weight… has the effect of holding the back end down during sharp changes of direction, so that there is less evidence of camber change, even though the suspension geometry is unaltered.'

Car and Driver was very enthusiastic about the new model, even forgiving its poor ventilation as a British sports-car tradition. It never quite adjusted to the low-geared steering, and found the controls rather dead. But the GT6 was 'an extremely good car, much improved over any previous Triumph offering.' It was 'an almost perfect car for the beginning sports car enthusiast who insists upon a small car with good performance and two seats.' Indeed, the GT6 was 'found wanting in only two or three areas – the interior was cramped, the shift linkage and clutch engagement were slow, and the ride was pitchy and harsh on rough surfaces.'

PRODUCTION CHANGES

Not many changes were made to the GT6 during its first two years of production, and most of those paralleled changes made on the Mk 3 Spitfire at the same time. Thus there were brake modifications, first of all as smaller rear-wheel cylinders were fitted to give better braking balance and then when a ratchet-type handbrake replaced the original fly-off type. Then there were changes to the door locks, when the key-locks gained double-entry keys and stronger, anti-burst locks were fitted. Unique to the six-cylinder engine, however (although shared with other cars that used it), was a change to a stronger crankshaft with larger main bearings.

Paint and trim colours, GT6 Mk 1

October 1966 – January 1967
There were five exterior and three interior colours. The combinations available were the same as for the final Spitfire Mk 2 models and were:

Body colour	Upholstery colour
Conifer Green (25)	black
Royal Blue (56)	black or Midnight Blue
Signal Red (32)	black
Wedgwood Blue (26)	Midnight Blue
White (19)	black or red

February 1967 – September 1968
There were five exterior and three interior colours. The combinations available were:

Body colour	Upholstery colour
Conifer Green	black
Royal Blue	black or Midnight Blue
Signal Red	black
Wedgwood Blue	Midnight Blue
White	black or red

RIVALS

As is so often the case with a successful car, the GT6's makers pitched it into a market where there was almost no competition. As announced in October 1966, the car was priced at £800 in the United Kingdom, plus purchase tax. This was exactly the same price as Triumph's own TR4A soft top and cheaper than the directly comparable MGB GT at £825. Morgan could supply a Plus 4 two-seater Coupé for £780, but this was by no means a readily-available, mass-production car. By the time of the 1967 Earls Court Show, the GT6's basic price remained unchanged. The MGB GT, however, cost more (£888.10s) and the TR4A had been replaced by a six-cylinder TR5 which was much more expensive at £985.

The GT6 was priced at about the same level as the better-equipped or more sporting 1.5-litre saloons of the time. Thus the MG Magnette with automatic transmission cost £811.10s in 1966, while a Sunbeam Rapier cost £750 and a Riley 4/72 was £760.10s. A Humber Sceptre cost £850. There were bigger saloons from the cheaper manufacturers, of course: Vauxhall's Cresta cost £809.17s, while Ford would supply a Zephyr V6 for just £832.

Performance figures: GT6 Mk 1

The Mk 1 GT6 would run to around 105mph (168km/h) when equipped with overdrive; the taller-geared, non-overdrive cars were capable of similar maximum speeds but reached them rather more slowly. From a standing start, the overdrive model took about 12 sec to reach 60mph. The fuel consumption of both types was normally around 20–22mpg (14.1–12.9l/100km).

---

4   Spitfire Mk 3 (1967–70)

While the Spitfire 4 Mk 2 had been on sale Triumph had been beavering away to improve the car, and when a new model was announced at the beginning of March 1967 – in time for the Geneva Motor Show that month – it incorporated a number of important new features. Many of them, such as the higher front bumper mounting and the improved soft top, were the result of American market demands. The new model was known as the Spitfire Mk 3, and the '4' in the name had been dropped. This

By the time the Spitfire Mk 3 was introduced in March 1967 it was D-suffix registration time in Great Britain. JDU 24 D was the much-photographed publicity car and here shows quite clearly the raised bumper which reminded some people of the Lotus Elan.

has never been fully explained, but it was probably done because the six-cylinder GT6 was then on sale and there was no longer any need to emphasize that the Spitfire had a four-cylinder engine.

The key features of the Spitfire Mk 3 were better performance from a larger-capacity, 1,296cc engine, uprated brakes to match this and a proper convertible top instead of the crude do-it-yourself type which had rapidly dated the early cars. This had a slightly different profile from

the earlier type, and was tensioned by a pair of over-centre catches of the type used on the Herald convertible. The windscreen frame also changed to suit, its capping being narrower and lacking the retaining lip for the earlier soft top. A related change was the addition of rain guttering on each windscreen pillar, although it seems probable that this was actually introduced on the final Mk 2 Spitfires and was not new for the Mk 3.

While the overall styling remained

The rear bumper was also higher up on the Mk 3, as this side view of the car demonstrates.

Identification and production: Spitfire Mk 3

The Commission Number of a Spitfire Mk 3 is in the same place as on earlier models. The numbering sequences are:

FD1 to FD 15306
FD 20000 to FD 51967
FD75000 to FD 92803
(FD ....U numbers were used on later Federal Mk 3s)

In theory, therefore, there were 65,076 Mk 3 models, made up of 15,306 in the first sequence, 31,967 in the second and 17,803 in the third. It is unfortunately not possible to tie these figures up with annual production figures which are organized by calendar year and do not differentiate between Mk 3, Mk IV and US-model 1500s during 1973 and 1974. The claimed production figure generally recognized for Mk 3s is 65,320.

Spitfire Mk 3 engines have numbers prefixed by FD, by FE (1970 Federal types with a single Zenith-Stromberg carburettor), or by FF (for Puerto Rico). Gearboxes also have an FD prefix. However, the final drives carry the same FC prefix as was used for the Mk 1 and Mk 2 cars.

unchanged, there was also a reworked front end, with the bumper now raised by 9in to run across the grille and meet new American regulations. This bumper also had new over-riders, which were now rubber-faced, and underneath it were combined indicator/sidelamp clusters instead of the separate round lamps of earlier Spitfires. Behind it was a wider front grille made of aluminium, which was the same as that used on the Mk 1 GT6 but with the spaces between the segments painted black. The Triumph shield was also no longer fitted on the bonnet.

The rear quarter-bumpers were also raised and no longer carried over-riders, and there were now twin circular reversing lamps just inboard of the indicator lamps. These were larger than they had been on earlier cars and were fitted slightly higher than before. The badging had changed, too, with the '4' being omitted from the Spitfire script and 'Mk 3' replacing the chromed Mk 2 badge.

Changes had also been made inside the vehicle, although Triumph had clearly decided that this was not the time to spend money on standardizing the heater or on relocating the instruments. These were still stuck in the middle of the facia, but their appearance had been improved with a wooden surround panel, and the speedometer now read (optimistically) to 120mph (193km/h) instead of 110mph (177km/h). More welcome, and more valuable, was the switch to a 15in wire-spoke steering wheel, which made a big improvement over the 16in Herald saloon type fitted to earlier Spitfires. Essentially the same as the TR4A type, it nevertheless had a plastic rim instead of the leather-bound rim of the more expensive car. Invisible until the bonnet was opened was the fact that the electrical system had now been changed from the old positive-earth type to the negative-earth type which was becoming the norm and suited the radios and other electrical equipment now becoming available.

There was much more to the new 1,296cc engine than an over-bored 1,147cc block fitted with new pistons. When the 1,296cc engine had been introduced in the front-wheel drive Triumph 1300 in October 1965, it was given a developed version of the eight-port head used on the competition Spitfires. The inlet port shape on the competition engines had been compromised by the need to avoid the head fixing studs, but on the Mk 3 engine the port shape was optimized and the fixing studs were altered, being reduced in number from eleven to ten at the same time. The block, of course, had to be retooled to suit.

To suit the larger bore, the combustion chambers in the head were enlarged and Triumph took the opportunity to fit inlet and exhaust valves of larger diameter. These were spaced further apart than before, with the result that the push-rods also had to be relocated. To simplify manufacture, their tubes were incorporated into the new cylinder head casting, and so the Spitfire engine lost its distinctive, separate, push-rod tubes.

Thus both block and head were new to the Spitfire. The outrigger-type rocker shaft end pedestals were also taken from the 1300 engine. External differences could be seen too in the water-heated, four-port, inlet manifold and in the disc-shaped emissions-control valve mounted on the manifold. This was part of a new closed-circuit crankcase breathing system which sucked crankcase fumes directly into the inlet manifold in order to prevent the air filters from becoming clogged. A cast-iron exhaust manifold replaced the fabricated type of the Mk 2 1,147cc engine, and this was more rigid than the old type, providing better support for the inlet manifold which rested on it. The exhaust system was also new, with a bigger 1⅝in outside diameter and silencers based on the GT6 type. On earlier Spitfires it had emerged under the centre of the rear bumper, but to meet regulations in some export territories it was rerouted on the Mk 3 to emerge under the right-hand side at the rear.

The end result of all these changes were a power increase to 75bhp at 6,000rpm (the Mk 2 had 67bhp at 6000rpm) and a torque increase to 75lb.ft at 4,000rpm (from 67lb.ft at 3,750rpm). To deal with the improved torque, the clutch was fitted with a stronger diaphragm spring than before, and to ensure that the brakes were still up to their job, larger front disc calipers were installed. These were Girling 14LF Mk 3 types, which offered both a small increase in swept area and greater pad volume to give a longer service life and less fade. And, perhaps to improve the handling, stiffer front road-springs were fitted.

WHAT THE BRITISH PRESS SAID

The earliest road test of a Mk 3 Spitfire published in a major motoring magazine was *Autosport*'s, in its issue of 21 April 1967. John Bolster had driven a car from Le Touquet in France down to the Geneva Motor Show – a jaunt laid on by the Triumph press office in which several motoring journalists participated – and he was very impressed. He summarized the Spitfire Mk 3 as 'an attractive little car with plenty of speed and remarkable fuel economy. It is better sprung than most small sports cars, though stronger dampers might not come amiss in France.'

Poor French roads did cause the suspension to bottom and the new brakes required high pedal pressures for emergency stops. Nevertheless, 105mph (168km/h) was indicated more than once on the speedometer (probably optimistically, it must be said) and the 36mpg (7.9l/100km) or so achieved in hard driving with two up plus luggage was an excellent return. Bolster thought the car was very cosy in its hardtop form,

---

Performance figures: Spitfire Mk 3

The 1,296cc Mk 3 Spitfire was not dramatically faster than its 1,147cc forebears if paper figures are to be believed. Nevertheless, it undoubtedly felt faster on the road. The maximum speed was about 95mph (152km/h) and, as before, the best that could be achieved with overdrive engaged was a few miles per hour less than that. Acceleration from standstill to 60mph (100km/h) took about 14.5 sec – a whole second less than a Mk 2 car – and similar gains in acceleration were observable right through the speed range. The bigger engine in the lightweight body gave the Mk 3 an even better fuel consumption, however, and figures of up to 40mpg (7.1l/100km) could be achieved.

At this stage, the modifications made to Federal cars did not greatly affect performance. The early Federal Mk 3 Spitfires should in theory, therefore, have been as fast as their non-Federalized counterparts.

---

but observed that it did tend to mist up.

When *Motor* tested a Mk 3 for its issue of 19 August 1967, it pointed out that the character of the Spitfire depended on the options and accessories fitted to it. The test car had a hardtop, heater, overdrive, wire wheels and radial tyres – and the combined cost of all those took the car out of the inexpensive sports-car category and into the next one up. Even so, the heating system was crude and lacked an air-volume control, and it would have been helpful to have had an interior light. In its comfort and in the range of seat adjustment available, however, the Spitfire was 'superior to most other cars of its type and price'.

Fuel consumption was outstandingly good at 32.8mpg (8.63l/100km), not least because the test team had been driving the car hard. However, the engine's low-speed flexibility was poor and the sudden throttle action needed acclimatization. The engine was smooth enough up to 5,500rpm, but became rougher and noisier above that. Gear ratios and the final drive were low for a sports car and the overdrive solenoid was sluggish in action.

The steering was direct enough, but seemed to lack the precision and sensitivity expected of a sports car. The handling was

otherwise quite sound, although the tail could hop out of line when a bumpy bend caught the short-travel suspension out. *Motor* also drew attention firmly to the tricky behaviour of the swing-axles. One tester had lost the car when the tail had come around, but had been quick enough to catch it. Another one was not so lucky, and had 'lost the car completely on the inner circuit at MIRA.... Prospective owners should make sure that they can cope with this behaviour which might very occasionally be elicited by extreme emergency avoiding action on the road.'

When *Autocar* tested a Mk 3 Spitfire for its 16 May 1968 issue it was more forgiving of the handling. To be fair, this was not a full road test, but the test team seem to have tried hard with the car. They described the swing-axles as 'mischievous' but argued that the transition to oversteer which would occur if the driver lifted off the throttle in mid-corner was 'without viciousness and drama'. On wet roads things would happen much more quickly, but the driver would know what to expect and should be able to cope with it.

There were some negative points, notably that the body seemed to flex a lot in comparison with a saloon car, and the testers flatly stated that the 'instrument sitings are all bad'. Nevertheless, the Spitfire Mk 3 'has all the ingredients which make driving fun and that is exactly what sports cars are for.' The 1,296cc engine was smooth and asked to be revved, and it had enough bottom-end torque to permit the use of second gear when crawling in traffic, so that the absence of synchromesh on first was not a problem.

Yet when *Autocar* pitted a Spitfire Mk 3 against an MG Midget in a comparison test for its issue of 10 April 1969, it printed some truly alarming photographs of the swing-axle oversteer which contrasted dramatically with those of the MG's tidy cornering. While the comparative test did not reveal any startling new truths, it did reveal that the two small sports cars had quite different characters. The Spitfire was the more comfortable and relaxing car and the better one for long-distance work. But the testers inclined towards preferring the Midget, which would certainly not have been the case five or six years earlier.

PRODUCTION CHANGES TO THE SPITFIRE MK 3

Spitfire development remained a continuous process and minor modifications continued to appear during the production life of the Mk 3. One of the strangest was the deletion of the engine valances at FD16351 and their relegation to being an extra-cost option once again. Perhaps this was one of the penny-pinching moves for which British Leyland's accountants were to become famous. The cooling-system pressure was increased from 7 to 13psi and the radiator and hoses were changed to suit. The fly-off handbrake was switched for a conventional ratchet type, smaller-diameter rear-wheel brake cylinders were fitted and there were improved anti-burst door locks. The nearside wiper was moved outboard of the washer jet and its arm was modified to suit and the optional wire wheels also lost their eared spinners, which were replaced by hexagonal items in line with the safety-conscious thinking of the times.

There were also a number of changes to

Factory-installed options: Spitfire Mk 3

Alternator (to replace dynamo)
Door mirror for driver's side
Engine valances (from FD 16351)
Grease nipples for upper ball joints and track rod ends
Heater
Laminated windscreen
Leather upholstery
Overdrive
Radial tyres (Dunlop Gold Seal SP41, 145 × 13)
Skid plate
Steering-column lock
Sun visors
Tonneau cover (in black or white only)
Whitewall tyres (5.20 × 13 crossply)

There were further revisions on 1970 models. The dark paintwork of this car makes it hard to pick out the matt black windscreen-surround panel. The bonnet, correctly, does not have chromed Triumph lettering across its nose but the small rectangular name badge which should be offset to the passenger side is missing.

the soft top and the hardtop. The linings of both were also changed: the original white hardtop lining was changed to beige and then to black, and the hood lining was changed from beige (with a beige-painted metal frame) to black (with a black-painted frame). Lever-type catches for the soft top replaced the over-centre Herald type and, in the same area, the hood well was given a PVC cover which matched the interior trim and was attached to the body by press studs.

The Spitfire had always outsold the BMC Sprite and Midget twins until 1969, when the position was reversed. It was this which prompted Triumph to introduce a

facelift package for the 1970 season which began in October 1969 – and with the desired success, because in 1970 the Spitfire once again outsold its two domestic rivals.

The enhanced cars were numbered in a new sequence, beginning with FD 75000, and they were most easily recognizable by their matt black windscreen surrounds and by the single reversing lamp, which was now incorporated within a new number-plate lamp shroud. The grilles were also finished in matt black (although they were less obvious since they were partly concealed behind the front bumper) and there were new plate badges in the latest corpo-

The 1970 models also brought a cleaned-up rear end. This picture shows the new lamp unit across the rear, incorporating number-plate lamps and a central reversing lamp; the Triumph plate badge can also be seen. This boot-mounted luggage rack was an optional extra.

rate style. The one on the bonnet read 'Spitfire', and the Triumph name was no longer displayed at the front of the car at all. On the boot lid there was no longer a script Spitfire badge, but instead the plate badge carried the Triumph name. Interior changes were confined to a GT6-style steer-ing wheel with flat spokes and to the addi-tion of knee-pads on either side of the centre console, like those already fitted to the Mk 3s marketed in the USA. In addi-tion, the soft top was now equipped with a zip-in rear window, and 4.5in wheel rims were standardized.

The dashboard remained unchanged when the 1970 models were introduced, except for the substitution of this flat-spoked steering wheel for the earlier wire-spoked type.

Triumph Spitfire Mk 3 (1967–70)

Layout
All-steel bodyshell bolted to steel backbone-frame chassis; two-seater open sports car, with front engine and rear-wheel drive.

Engine

Block material	cast iron
Head material	cast iron
Cylinders	four, in line
Cooling	water
Bore and stroke	73.7mm × 76mm (2.90in × 2.99in)
Capacity	1,296cc (79.1 cu.in)
Valves	overhead, two per cylinder
Compression ratio	9.0:1
	1969 US models: 8.5:1
	1970 US models: 9.0:1
Carburettors	two SU type HS2 (1.25in)
	1970 US models: single Stromberg type 150 CDSE
Max. power	75bhp at 6,000rpm
	1969–70 US models: 68bhp at 5,500rpm
Max. torque	75lb.ft at 4,000rpm
	1969–70 US models: 73lb.ft at 3,000rpm

Transmission
Hydraulically-operated diaphragm clutch with 6.5in diameter; four-speed, manual gearbox with synchromesh on 2nd, 3rd and 4th gear only, and optional overdrive (Laycock D-type).

Gearbox ratios

Top	1.00:1
Third	1.39:1
Second	2.16:1
First	3.75:1
Reverse	3.75:1
Overdrive	0.802:1
Final drive ratio	4.11:1

Suspension and steering

Front	independent, with twin wishbones, coil springs, anti-roll bar and telescopic dampers
Rear	independent, with swing-axles, radius arms, transverse leaf spring and telescopic dampers
Steering	rack and pinion, with 3.75:1 ratio
Tyres	5.20 × 13 crossply
Wheels	four-stud steel type standard
	centre-lock wire type optional
Rim width	3.5in (steel wheels) or 4.5in (wire type); steel wheels with 4.5in rims from FD 75000 (1970 model-year)

Triumph Spitfire Mk 3 (1967–70) *(continued)*

Brakes

Type	discs at the front
	drums at the rear
Size	disc diameter 9in
	drum diameter 7in, width 1.25in

Dimensions [in(mm)]

Wheelbase	83(2,108)
Track, front	49(1,245)
Track, rear	48(1,220)
Overall length	147(3,734)
Overall width	57(1,448)
Overall height	47.5(1,206)
Unladen weight	1,568lb(711kg)

A Mk 3 milestone

The 100,000th Spitfire to be built was a Mk 3 model. It was a Jasmine Yellow car for the British market, and left the assembly lines in February 1968.

A big occasion: the 100,000th Spitfire came off the production lines on 8 February 1968. Standing in the middle, wearing a suit, is George Turnbull, Triumph's general manager. Along with the engineering chief Harry Webster, he was soon to go to the Austin-Morris volume-cars division.

Dealer accessories: Spitfire Mk 3

Some of these accessories were approved aftermarket items and were not manufactured specifically for the Spitfire.

Anti-mist panel for hardtop
Bonnet lock
Boot rack (fixed type)
Boot rack (removable type)
Brake servo (Girling Powerstop)
Cigarette lighter
Competition front springs
Competition rear springs
Continental touring kit
Door buffer with reflector
Electric defroster
Emergency windscreen
Exhaust tailpipe finisher
Floor mats (rubber)
Fog lamp (quartz–iodine type)
Fuel-pipe filter
Hardtop
Headlamp mask (to give right-hand dip for Continental touring)
Hub-cap medallion
Hub-cap removal tool
Instrument mounting panel for single auxiliary gauge
Instrument mounting panel for two auxiliary gauges
Locking petrol-filler cap
Mudflaps (rear wheels only)
Oil cooler
Paints (touch-in)
Safety-warning triangle
Seat belts (inertia-reel Kangol type)
Seat belts (static, three-point type)
Sill protectors
Soft top conversion kit (for cars supplied with hardtop only)
Spark-plug spanner (Plugmaster type)
Spark plugs (Champion UN12Y)
Spot lamp (quartz–iodine type)
Steering-wheel glove (brown leather or simulated leather)
Tow bar
Tow rope and luggage-rack strap
Wheelbrace (Lever Master type)
Wheel trim rings
Wing mirror (thirteen different types were available)
Wing-mirror extension (for towing)
Wire wheels with 4.5in rim (supplied with eared spinner up to FD 11732 and with hexagonal spinner thereafter)
Wooden gear-lever knob
Wood-rim steering wheel

Special Tuning

Marketing of the competition accessories which Triumph offered for the Spitfire was transferred during 1969 to the British Leyland Special Tuning department, which was established in the old BMC Competitions Department at Abingdon. By September 1969, when *Cars and Car Conversions* magazine reported on what could be achieved, no fewer than eighteen bolt-on items were listed. All could be ordered through Triumph distributors.

The Special Tuning demonstrator was a 1968 Mk 3 Spitfire registered as LHP 221 F, which had earlier seen service as a press demonstrator. It was fitted with 5.5J wheels, a brake servo, twin 1.5in SU carburettors with an accelerator cable kit, a competition exhaust manifold, a thirteen-row oil cooler and an accelerator kit. The whole was set off by Special Tuning emblems on the bodywork – rare items today.

Cars and Car Conversions considered that the accelerator cable conversion was one of the best items, as it offered a much smoother accelerator action than the standard type. On test, the Special Tuning demonstrator reached an indicated 110mph (177km/h) on a couple of occasions, and its 0–60mph (100km/h) time was down to 11.9 sec from the 13.4 of the standard Mk 3. The wide wheels and radial tyres allowed much higher cornering speeds than on the standard car, but it was still possible to provoke the swing-axles into oversteer.

THE FEDERAL SPITFIRES, 1969–70

The Spitfire had enjoyed enormous and well-deserved success in the USA in the first half of the 1960s and it was in the USA where the great majority of all Spitfires had been sold. The car remained a well-respected and much liked machine, its limitations known and acknowledged and – as often as not – largely countered by after-market modifications. However, the mid-1960s saw the beginnings of a movement in the USA which would eventually change the face of the car market in that country for ever and would force a number of unwelcome modifications upon the Spitfire which eventually sealed its fate.

There were, in fact, two separate issues being hotly debated at that time in America. The first was the question of automotive safety, the debate on which had been initated by Ralph Nader's book *Unsafe at any speed,* in which he singled out the Chevrolet Corvair as a car which handled badly and could cause inexperi-

enced drivers to lose control. The Corvair was the focus of Nader's thesis, but he struck out at other models, too. The book served as ammunition for consumer pressure groups, which persuaded the Federal government to introduce the first of a series of legally-enforceable safety standards for all vehicles sold in the country. The first Federal safety standards were announced in 1966 and were due to become law during 1968.

The second issue which then concerned the car makers was that of air pollution. Airborne pollution was recognized to create health problems, especially in major cities such as Los Angeles, and an important cause of this pollution had been determined to be vehicle emissions (other major sources of it being industry and domestic fuel burning). What matters is that the legislators clamped down on the amount of noxious gases permitted in car exhausts in the Clean Air Act of 1967. Once again, the car makers had to clean up their act – this time literally – beginning in 1968.

The Federal safety standards had little

The bumper height had been changed to suit North American demands; this is a 1968-model Spitfire Mk 3 for the USA, wearing the wheeltrims used only on North American cars. Note that the soft top also differs from the type used on earlier models.

effect on the Spitfire at first, but the exhaust emissions regulations did and their result was damaging to the car in the long term, as the regulations themselves were tightened. The real problem was that the only way of reducing emissions to acceptable levels was by a series of measures which reduced power and performance, and generally took away from the Spitfire a lot of the sportiness which was its *raison d'être*. It was fortunate for Triumph that all manufacturers selling in the USA during the late 1960s suffered from the same problems, but there is little doubt that this loss of performance was a major factor in the later collapse of the market for British sports cars in the USA.

The first Federalized Spitfires were those for the 1969 model-year. They had redesigned seats with large, fixed head restraints and the side of each front wing carried an amber marker-light while there was a corresponding red one on each rear wing. These measures were designed to improve safety: the headrests to prevent whiplash injuries in a collision and the marker lights to make the cars more visible from the side at night. There was also a completely different dashboard, covered in matt black leathercloth and with the instruments sensibly placed directly in front of the driver. Knee padding on either side of the centre console was intended to reduce injuries in an accident but was wel-

In 1969, the British Leyland importers in the USA ran a contest in which participants were asked to come up with paintwork ideas. Known as the Great Rover / Triumph car painting competition, it promised eight winners the opportunity to see their work translated into reality. This Spitfire Mk 3 was painted to a design by Jeffrey Pasco of San Francisco. Whitewall tyres, side marker lights and those special wheel trims were all standard features and were testimony to the growing gulf between American models and those for the rest of the world.

come also as a more comfortable leg rest, and a small fuel expansion tank fitted in the boot behind the right-hand wheelarch was supposed to catch any fuel displaced from the main tank in an accident and to prevent the sort of spillage which could lead to a fire.

To reduce emissions, the engines were fitted with a PCV valve, readily visible on top of the inlet manifold just above the rear carburettor. This in turn demanded a lower compression ratio to avoid misfiring, so the Federal Spitfires for 1969 had an 8.5:1 compression instead of the 9.0:1 standard for the rest of the world. The result, inevitably, was a loss of engine efficiency and so also a loss of power and performance. At this stage, however, the losses were not too great: Federal engines were rated at 68bhp (as opposed to the 75bhp tune for other

Paint and trim colours: Spitfire Mk 3

All cars had the code numbers of their original body and trim colours stamped on to their Commission Number plates.

February 1967 – August 1968
There were five exterior and three interior colours; the combinations available were:

Body colour	*Upholstery colour*
Conifer Green	black
Royal Blue	black or Midnight Blue
Signal Red	black
Wedgwood Blue	Midnight Blue
White	black or red

September 1968 – August 1969
The number of exterior colours was increased to eight by the introduction of three new ones; the previous season's five remained available; there were now four trim colours; only black remained of the previous season's three; the options were:

Body colour	*Upholstery colour*
Conifer Green	black or Matador Red
Damson Red	black or tan
Jasmine Yellow	black or tan
Royal Blue	black or Shadow Blue
Signal Red	black or tan
Valencia Blue	black or tan
Wedgwood Blue	black or Shadow Blue
White	black, Matador Red or tan

September 1969 – April 1970
The number of interior colours went up to nine; two were new and Conifer Green had been dropped; the four trim colours were the same as those available during the previous season; the options were:

Body colour	*Upholstery colour*
Damson Red	black or tan
Jasmine Yellow	black or tan
Laurel Green	black or Matador Red
Royal Blue	black or Shadow Blue
Sienna Brown	black or tan
Signal Red	black or tan
Valencia Blue	black or tan
Wedgwood Blue	black or Shadow Blue
White	black, Matador Red or tan

Paint and trim colours: Spitfire Mk3 *(continued)*

May – December 1970
There were still nine colours, although Jasmine Yellow had been dropped; in its place came:

Body colour	Upholstery colour
Saffron Yellow	black or tan

---

markets) and produced 73lb.ft of torque as against 75lb.ft elsewhere. American motoring magazines were wary of quoting performance figures in these years in case they were accused of encouraging drivers to drive irresponsibly, but a 1969 Federal Mk 3 Spitfire took about 15 sec to reach 60mph from rest and, when fully extended, was probably only a little short of the 95mph (152km/h) maximum promised by other Mk 3s at this time.

Besides, Triumph had managed to draw buyers' attention away from the performance losses with some cosmetic items. As in other markets, there were three new paint and three new trim colours and in addition to these the American market had new wheel covers. These were once again full-size items with a vaned outer section, but this time they had a dished centre section with the Spitfire name in capital letters around it. As an extra-cost alternative, American buyers could have some striking spoked magnesium-alloy racing wheels in the fashion of the day, and all American cars had tyres with a thin whitewall stripe. Neither type of wheel was available in other markets and nor were the whitewalls – at least, not as original equipment.

For the 1970 season the Federal Spitfires remained visually unchanged, but there were engine modifications. In order to meet the emissions regulations, the twin SU carburettors were replaced by a single Stromberg (a type specially developed for emissions-controlled engines). Triumph did put the compression ratio back up to 9.0:1, and the power and the torque output remained as they had been for 1969. But nobody was fooled: no single-carburettor installation ever offered the same responsiveness as a multiple-carburettor set-up, and the 1970 Federal models had certainly lost something.

Yet no one complained too much either. Perhaps Americans were only too pleased that they could still buy a genuine British roadster with sporting pretensions at a time when new regulations seemed to be threatening traditional perceptions of the car. When *Road Test* put a 1969 model through its paces for its February issue that year, it concluded that the Spitfire 'has gotten smoother, quieter and more comfortable with age, and the price is still bargain basement'. A camber compensator was still an 'absolutely necessary accessory' and the new head restraints made erection of the soft top more difficult than before. Fuel economy remained excellent, luggage space poor but the interior offered more comfort than was to be expected of a small roadster even though access was a problem for the long-legged. There was not a single complaint about performance; 'Spitfires are fun', the magazine concluded.

5 GT6 Mk 2 and GT6+ (1968–70)

It was quite clear to anyone who read the road tests of the original GT6 that the car had a great deal of merit but also some serious flaws. The main ones which these early tests highlighted were the misbehaviour of the swing-axle rear suspension and the poor passenger-cabin ventilation. Yet, strangely enough, the customers seem to have been happy with the car, and there seems to have been no pressure on the Triumph engineering department to make any major modifications.

Nevertheless, there were many more vociferous complaints about the rear suspension of the Vitesse 2-litre, which had been launched at the same time as the GT6 in October 1966. This car had the same powertrain as the GT6, and its higher centre of gravity and greater weight threw the shortcomings of the rear suspension into greater relief. Triumph was most certainly obliged to do something about this as soon as possible, and the decision was made that the modified rear suspension needed by the Vitesse should also be used to improve the GT6.

The Mk 2 version of the GT6 was distinguished by its raised bumper, by chromed louvres behind the quarter-windows and by fake Rostyle wheel trims. This left-hand drive example was probably destined for Switzerland; note the single and rather unattractive wing mirror on the driver's side.

The enthusiastic owner of this 1969 model has fitted contemporary Minilite wheels in place of the factory originals. The bonnet side louvres unique to the Mk 2 models can be seen clearly here.

There already existed several cures for the lift-off oversteer associated with the swing-axles, although many of them were suitable for competition use only because they depended on stiffer springing which ruined the ride quality of the car. It appears that the Triumph engineers had already devised the 'swing-spring' arrangement which would eventually go into production on the Spitfire Mk IV in 1970, but Harry Webster's engineers thought that they could do better for the Vitesse and the GT6. The strut-type suspension designed for the stillborn GT6R racer (see Chapter 9) was going to demand too many expensive modifications to the rest of the

car, and so that was rejected as well. The design eventually chosen was inspired by the Formula 1 Cooper of the late 1950s, and was first built and tested by the Triumph competitions department during 1967.

The new suspension retained the transverse leaf spring, but this now doubled as an upper wishbone. Meanwhile, new driveshafts were fitted, incorporating a large, rubber Rotoflex coupling near their outer ends. This coupling, already familiar from the front-wheel drive 1300 saloon, allowed a certain amount of articulation as well as cushioning the driveline against torsional shocks. Shaped to fit around this large cou-

> **Performance figures: GT6 Mk 2**
>
> An overdrive-equipped GT6 Mk 2 was capable of around 107mph (171km/h) and 0–60mph (100km/h) in about 10 sec. Fuel consumption was a little short of 30mpg (9.4l/100km) overall, but depended to some extent on the driver's style.
>
> The GT6 +, or Federal version of the car, would reach around 105mph (168km/h) and took just under 12 sec to accelerate to 60mph from rest. Fuel consumption was between 22 and 25 miles per US gallon.

pling were new, lower wishbones which ran between the chassis frame and the wheels; they were described as 'reversed' wishbones, because they had two pivots at the wheel ends and a single one on the chassis. Meanwhile, the radius-arm pivot pick-ups were moved nearer to the centre of the car, and the mountings for the telescopic dampers were relocated so that the dampers would not foul the Rotoflex coupling.

The result was a great improvement. The roll-height of the suspension was reduced by a full 6.5in, and the new arrangement worked much like a conventional twin-wishbone suspension. Camber change was minimized in cornering, so that the outer wheel no longer tucked under the car and the suspension no longer jacked up to the detriment of traction. Triumph had finally got it right.

The problem of cockpit ventilation in the GT6 was addressed too. Ventilation had always been a problem from the beginning, when experience with the original Michelotti fastback prototype and with the works racers and rally cars had led Triumph to fit the production cars with quarter-lights in the doors and opening rear side-windows. However, the main difficulty with this rather crude arrangement was that proper ventilation was available only with the windows open. It was also true that the six-cylinder engine generated much more heat than the Spitfire's four-cylinder type, and that this heat tended to find its way back into the passenger compartment, thus highlighting the poor through-flow of air.

The solution surprised no one. A heater was standardized at last, with a twin-speed fan instead of the single-speed type of the earlier optional heater, and with it came a proper cold-air ventilation system. This ducted air into the passenger compartment through a pair of Triumph 2000-style, face-level eyeball vents in the dashboard, and a pair of similar vents in the footwells kept the occupants' legs cool when necessary too. Air extraction was taken care of by louvred vents in the sides of the fastback, behind the windows, and the problem of heat coming in from the engine bay was tackled by fitting extractor louvres to the sides of the bonnet just behind the wheel arches. It all worked rather well.

The improved rear suspension and ventilation were strictly 'corrections' to the original design; but there were also improvements to the engine and changes to the transmission specification. The engine changes were brought about mainly through a process of rationalization with the 2.5-litre engine which had been introduced for the TR5 and TR250 in autumn 1967. This had incorporated not only a longer stroke but also a redesigned cylinder head with larger inlet and exhaust valves to give better breathing. As with the head on the 1,296cc four-cylinder engine, this

The Mk 2 cars came with these rather smart white enamel badges on the bonnet...

...and on the tail.

The eyeball air vents on the smart wooden dashboard make clear that this left-hand-drive interior is of a GT6 Mk 2.

one also had integral pushrod tubes instead of the separate ones of the earlier 2-litre cylinder head.

This new cylinder head was added to the GT6's 2-litre engine, together with the inlet manifold from the carburettor TR250 engine. The block was also modified, with a new crankshaft running in larger bearings, while a more sporty camshaft gave higher lift and longer overlap. Despite a slightly lower compression ratio of 9.25:1 (with which 100-octane fuel was no longer mandatory), the revised GT6 engine put out 104bhp instead of the 95 of the Mk 1 type, and its improved breathing was immediately apparent to anyone who drove it. The extra 9bhp put the car's top speed

up to around 110mph (177km/h).

One of the less worrying criticisms levelled at the early GT6 had been that the overdrive was largely redundant. The high 3.27:1 gearing of the non-overdrive car gave much the same overall gearing in top as the 3.89:1 overdrive model when the overdrive was engaged, so that the only advantage of the overdrive model was its better through-the-gears acceleration on the lower axle ratio. No one seemed to be too concerned about this, but Triumph decided to deliver all examples of the Mk 2 GT6 with the taller 3.27:1 gearing, whether equipped with overdrive or not. (Matters were different in the USA, however, as will be explained later.) However, the 3.27:1

Identification and production: GT6 Mk 2 and GT6+

The Commission Number of a GT6 Mk 2 or a GT6+ is in the same place as on earlier models. The numbering sequence for both cars was: KC 50001 to KC 83398.

There was a break in the numbering before the sequence started again at KC 75001 in October 1969. The actual production total for the Mk 2 and the GT6+ types combined was 12,066.

The engines have numbers prefixed by KC, or by KD in the case of emissions-controlled GT6+ types. Gearboxes also carry KC prefixes, while the final drive prefixes are KC for 3.27:1 types and KD for 3.89:1 types.

---

gearing was really too high for use with the overdrive, and cars with this gearing lacked any real accelerative ability when overdrive was engaged on top gear. Fortunately, the lower 3.89:1 axle ratio remained available to special order – and Triumph found itself dealing with a surprisingly large number of special orders.

There was one other change on the GT6 Mk 2 which was most definitely not for the better, and that was the switch from the neat Vitesse 1600-style wheel trims of the Mk 1 car to the dreadful imitation Rostyle wheel trims which were then in use on several other Triumph models. Wire wheels fortunately remained available, albeit at extra cost.

Other cosmetic changes brought the Mk 2 car's appearance into line with that of the Spitfire Mk 3, introduced some fifteen months earlier. Thus the front bumper was raised to halfway up the grille, and new lamp clusters incorporating both sidelights and indicators were fitted below it. The rear quarter-bumpers were also relocated above the lamps and larger rear indicator lenses were fitted, as on the Spitfire Mk 3. The windscreen wipers were more widely separated on the scuttle, as on the later Mk 3 Spitfires.

Nevertheless, the GT6 Mk 2 also had a number of unique features. Most obvious was its elegant plate badge, finished in cream enamel with the GT6 Mk 2 name

peeping through in bright metal. A stainless-steel finisher was fitted to the bottom of the sills, over a welded join, and there was also a distinctive new exhaust configuration. Instead of a centre silencer this now had a large silencer box mounted transversely just ahead of the rear valance. A similar layout would be adopted for the Spitfire Mk IV, some two years later.

Finally, Triumph had made a 15 ACR alternator standard and had made some worthwhile improvements inside the car. The wooden facia, modified to incorporate the eyeball air vents, now had a non-reflective matt finish instead of the polished finish of the Mk 1 cars. It also had a new, padded safety roll along its lower edge. The switchgear was now a flush-fitting type taken from the TR5 and the instruments all had black rather than chromed bezels. The seats had less padding to give a little more headroom, and three-point safety belts were now standard. There was also a new interior option, in the form of an occasional rear seat. To fit this it was necessary to remove the front section of the luggage floor and so to lose the cubby boxes underneath it. It has to be said that the seat was suitable only for small children who were too cowed to complain about their lot – but this new option did at least give the GT6 an additional weapon in the war against the MGB GT with its standard 2+2 configuration.

This, then, was the GT6 Mk 2 which made its bow in July 1968. That summer announcement, in time for the start of the 1969 model-year in the USA, indicated how much Triumph's schedules were geared to suit its best market across the Atlantic. Over there, of course, the new car was not actually called a GT6 Mk 2, but carried a different name ...

WHAT THE BRITISH PRESS SAID ABOUT THE GT6 MK 2

Although the British press reported on the introduction of the new GT6 Mk 2 in September 1968, it was not until the following spring that Triumph provided long-term loans of a press demonstrator car. Each of the three major British mgazines which tested the car was lent the same vehicle. Registered MWK 670 G, it was perhaps a little untypical of the standard British specification because it had the optional 3.89:1 axle with overdrive. This caused the *Motor* staff to become thoroughly confused in their report about which ratio was optional and which was standard.

The earliest of the three reports was published in *Autocar* on 3 April 1969. The test team found the engine flexibility much as before, and that the new cylinder head seemed to give better overall fuel economy. The maximum speed was 107mph (171km/h), a little better than the Mk 1's. However, improved acceleration was not discernible at

speeds below 50mph (80km/h). The front end of the car was too heavy and the steering still too low-geared, 'so it is still a car which needs learning before someone new to it can get the best from it. It would handle even better if it could be more evenly balanced like the Vitesse.' Most importantly, however, 'the back end feels so much more stable that it is hard to believe that so little has been done.'

In its issue dated 5 July 1969, *Motor* also complained of the low-geared steering and of the understeer resulting from the heavy front end. The ride was still rough on some surfaces, and the overall fuel consumption was no better than before; in fact, in touring conditions it was worse than for the Mk 1. The maximum speed was better, however, and the magazine recorded a best of 109.6mph (175km/h). Once again there was praise for the revised rear suspension:

> The new layout has banished the tendency to vicious oversteer that we had cause to criticise sharply in our last test and makes the GT6 a much safer and more predictable car. Nevertheless, we were a little disappointed in the roadholding which we don't regard as outstanding for an all-independent modern sports car.

The last of the major magazines to test a GT6 Mk 2 was *Autosport,* whose John Bolster claimed that the maximum speed was rather in excess of 110mph (177km/h). Perhaps MWK 670 G had loosened up more by this stage; certainly, each successive

---

The GT6 Mk 2 prototype

Triumph records list just one prototype of the Mk 2 GT6. This had the experimental Commission Number X 762, and is described as 'Revised wishbone Mk II, prototype IRS'. It was probably registered as PDU 446 E on 12 September 1967 and is recorded as having engine number 71579.

magazine to test it claimed a higher maximum speed! The improved roadholding was briefly acknowledged, and the car proved as lively as was to be expected. However, Bolster would have liked a brake servo. He complained that the transverse rear silencer looked like an afterthought and noted that, even though the heating and the ventilation were effective, some unwanted heat still came through the transmission tunnel in very hot weather. Finally, he detected a small fault which the other magazines had not: this was a tendency for the car to surge when crawling in low gear, which he ascribed to the Rotoflex couplings winding up and then unwinding.

THE GT6 + FOR THE USA

Marketing is a strange thing, and it was for marketing reasons that the revised GT6 was not called a GT6 Mk 2 in the USA but rather a GT6+. Presumably those reasons were sound ones, but they have never been fully explained even now. One way or another, however, the GT6+ carried the appropriate badges of a style similar to those on the Mk 2 model sold in Triumph's other markets.

Otherwise, the Federal car was not much different from the standard model. It differed from the North American GT6 Mk 1 in that wire wheels were now an extra-cost option rather than standard and, of course, it carried marker lamps on front and rear wings. Narrow-band, whitewall tyres were also part of the standard specification and the seats had built-in head restraints like those on the contemporary Federal Spitfires. The perforated vinyl used on the later reclining seats seems to have been introduced earlier on the non-reclining seats of Federal cars and was available by

This rather interesting picture is a 1969 publicity shot, showing a right-hand drive GT6 wearing the special wheel-trims used only on American models.

This American model is a proper left-hand drive GT6+. Note the side marker lights on front and rear wings. Just visible through the rear quarter-window is the fixed headrest of the US-market seat; the large transverse rear silencer can also be seen clearly.

The GT6+ sold in the USA had enamelled badges like the GT6 Mk 2s sold in other parts of the world.

Triumph GT6 Mk 2 (1968–70) and Triumph GT6 + (1968–70)

Layout
All-steel bodyshell bolted to steel backbone-frame chassis; two-seater fastback coupé, with front engine and rear-wheel drive.

Engine

Block material	cast iron
Head material	cast iron
Cylinders	six, in line
Cooling	water
Bore and stroke	74.7mm × 76mm (2.94in × 2.99in)
Capacity	1,998cc (122 cu.in)
Valves	overhead, two per cylinder
Compression ratio	9.25:1
Carburettors	two Zenith-Stromberg type 150 CD
Max. power	104bhp at 5,300rpm (GT6+ for USA, 95bhp at 4,700rpm)
Max. torque	117.3lb.ft at 3,000rpm (GT6+ for USA, 116.6lb.ft at 3,400rpm)

Transmission
Hydraulically-operated diaphragm clutch with 8.5in diameter; four-speed, all-synchromesh manual gearbox with optional overdrive (Laycock D-type).

Gearbox ratios

Top	1.00:1
Third	1.25:1
Second	1.78:1
First	2.65:1
Reverse	3.10:1
Overdrive	0.802:1
Final drive ratio	3.27:1 (3.89:1 on US models with overdrive, and to special order on overdrive models in other markets)

Suspension and steering

Front	independent, with twin wishbones, coil springs, anti-roll bar and telescopic dampers
Rear	independent, with reversed lower wishbones, radius arms, transverse leaf spring and telescopic dampers
Steering	rack and pinion, with 4.3:1 ratio
Tyres	155 SR 13 radial
Wheels	four-stud, steel type standard
	centre-lock wire type optional
Rim width	4.5in

Brakes

Type	discs at the front
	drums at the rear
Size	disc diameter 9.7in
	drum diameter 8in, width 1.25in

Dimensions [in(mm)]	
Wheelbase	83(2,108)
Track, front	49(1,245)
Track, rear	49(1,245)
Overall length	145(3,680)
Overall width	57(1,450)
Overall height	47(1,195)
Unladen weight	1,904lb(865kg)

about March 1969. There was also what contemporary advertisements called a 'self-sealing magnetic gas cap', a leather-covered gear knob, and eight-spoke magnesium-alloy wheels were available as an option.

WHAT THE AMERICAN PRESS SAID ABOUT THE GT6 +

Several American road tests of the GT6+ stressed what a bargain it was at $3,000. It was, said *Popular Imported Cars* in January 1969, 'the only $3000 GT car with the smoothness of a high performance engine and independent wishbone rear suspension'. The improved handling and ventilation earned almost universal praise, and the new heated rear window was also much liked; but the Americans were deeply suspicious of what might have been done to the engine to make it meet the latest exhaust-emissions regulations. There seemed to be no loss of performance, however, even though power was down from 104bhp to 95bhp, and the torque of 116.6lb.ft (as opposed to 117.3lb.ft) was generated at 3,400rpm instead of 3,000rpm.

That test by *Popular Imported Cars* was particularly enthusiastic, describing the GT6+ as 'even more fun to drive than its predecessor', thanks to its new rear suspension, and as 'one of the best-ventilated hard-top grand touring cars available – at any price'. In February 1969, *Road Test* magazine wittily noted that 'the things about it that are "+" are the very things that we found to be "–" last time we tested the car... the worst faults of the GT6 have become some of the greatest virtues of the GT6+'. The car was now a 'cornering demon. It not only performs but it handles too.'

However, some later road tests were much less enthusiastic. *Sports Car Graphic* found all kinds of faults in its March 1969 report, although acknowledging that the car was now much more stable on corners and that the new ventilation system was a great improvement. The brakes were heavy, the throttle unprogressive, the synchromesh beatable and reverse hard to select. The carburettors suffered from fuel starvation when cornering hard on a race-track and the higher of the two fan speeds caused a vibration in the footwell. Furthermore, there was a fault in the windscreen glass which distorted vision.

Car and Driver, in April 1969, was also very negative about the GT6+. The testers picked up again on the unprogressive throttle pedal and found the long travel of the brake pedal to be coupled to a sponginess in the brakes which left a feeling of insecurity. On the whole, the idea of putting the 2-litre engine into a fastback Spitfire shell had been a good one, but one which was poorly executed. Even the new suspension was not perfect, and 'the tail still likes to swing wide without much warning'. The cabin

---

Paint and trim colours: GT6 Mk 2 and GT6 +

The paint and trim colours and combinations available for the GT6 Mk 2 and GT6 + were identical to those of the contemporary Spitfire Mk 3. These combinations are listed in the tables in Chapter 4. Note that the GT6 Mk 2 and the GT6 + were introduced much later than the Spitfire Mk 3, and that the combinations listed under the period February 1967–August 1968 do not apply to the six-cylinder cars.

---

was cramped and the weld seams along the tops of the wings unforgivably cheapening. Over the standing quarter-mile, the GT6+ was 'still a long way behind the Datsun 2000 and little quicker than the Fiat 124 Spider'. Overall, it was 'a bleak, unfun [*sic*], hard-to-drive sports car – which is to say, no sports car at all.'

PRODUCTION CHANGES TO THE GT6 MK 2

Even though the GT6 Mk 2 was a much better car than its Mk 1 predecessor, it was, inexplicably, not rewarded with better sales. Over the two years of its production, however, it was not subjected to the stream of minor production modifications which affected the contemporary Spitfire Mk 3. Instead, Triumph saved a collection of changes up for the 1970 model-year and introduced these at the same time as a sim-

ilar package on the Spitfire.

The 1970 model-year changes incorporated some structural changes to meet new American collision-resistance requirements, particularly to the scuttle. Like the Spitfires, the 1970-model GT6s had a matt black windscreen surround panel and a single reversing lamp incorporated within the number-plate lamp shroud. They also took on the same matt black-painted radiator grilles (which were later changed to black plastic). Some late 1970 models had the Federal style of fuel filler-cap, although this was not fitted to the first of the modified cars.

Inside, the sides of the centre console were fitted with the knee-pads also seen on the Spitfire, and a new TR6-style steering wheel with bare instead of padded spokes was fitted. There were new seats, too, which reclined for the first time in a car of this family and had perforated Vynide coverings on their wearing surfaces. To give them room to move backwards, the front

---

Factory-installed options: GT6 Mk 2

Competition brake linings
Grease nipples for front upper ball joints
Grease nipples for track rod ends
Laminated windscreen
Leather upholstery and trim
Low-ratio (3.89:1) final drive for overdrive cars (except in the USA)
Overdrive
Skid plate
Steering-column lock

Dealer accessories: GT6 Mk 2

Anti-frost shield for windscreen
Bonnet locks
Brake servo (Girling Powerstop type)
Cigarette lighter (on bracket)
Continental touring kit
Electric defroster for windscreen
Emergency windscreen
Fire extinguisher
Fog lamp (Styla quartz–iodine type)
Fuel-tank filter
Luggage straps (pair, leather)
Mudflaps (rear wheels only)
Occasional rear seat
Oil cooler
Paints (touch-in)
Radio (Smith's Radiomobile) and aerial
Roof rack
Safety-warning triangle
Sill protectors
Spark-plug spanner (Plugmaster type)
Spot lamp (Styla quartz–iodine type)
Sunroof (Tudor Webasto folding type; fitted by specialists)
Tow bar
Tow rope and luggage-rack strap
Wheelbrace (Lever Master type)
Wing mirrors
Wire wheels (always supplied with hexagonal spinners)
Wood-rim steering wheel

section of the luggage floor was no longer fitted – but with it went the useful if rather inaccessible cubbies behind the seats.

RIVALS

The GT6 continued to undercut the price of its most obvious rival, the MGB GT, by a worthwhile amount. MG was by this stage fielding yet another version of its fastback sports tourer in the shape of the MGC GT; but this 3-litre-engined car was considerably more expensive than the Triumph and its handling was spoiled by a heavy front end. The Bond Equipe 2+2 GT also came into the picture and used what were essentially the underpinnings of Triumph's own Vitesse 2-litre. However, it was priced midway between the GT6 Mk 2 and the MGB GT and was always a low-volume model.

From 1969 many potential GT6 buyers might well have considered Ford's new Capri, which in its 2000GT form was cheaper than the GT6. For a price slightly above that of the MGB GT the tyre-smoking 3000GT version could be had, and this would certainly have been a tempting proposition for those whose budgets were not too severely constrained. After 1968 Opel's GT was also an interesting GT6 alternative, although it was available only with left-hand drive.

6   Spitfire Mk IV (1970–74)

British Triumph enthusiasts found it rather hard to understand the circumstances of the Spitfire Mk IV's launch in October 1970, and the background to it certainly takes a little explanation. As far as it is now possible to establish, the car's introduction – and that of its sister vehicle the GT6 Mk 3 – was actually intended to coincide with the start of the American model-year in January 1971. Production cars would not be obtainable before then, and the plan was for the new models to be made available simultaneously in all markets at the same time.

The problem was that, although the Detroit Motor Show in January would be an ideal launch platform in the USA, there were no comparable European motor shows at that time of the year. The London Motor Show in October 1970 would be too early

The restyled Mk IV models looked much sharper and more contemporary. This picture shows quite clearly the new lines of the bonnet and rear wings, together with the squared-up hardtop.

and, if the cars were launched there, Triumph would be faced with a pent-up demand by January which it might be unable to satisfy in the short term. So a decision was made that the new models would be launched at one of the continental European shows in the autumn. This would allow news of the cars to spread, but would delay demand in the United Kingdom until the new models were in full production.

Thus the Turin Motor Show was chosen for the announcement, probably on the grounds that Turin was the home town of Giovanni Michelotti, who was responsible for the styling of the new models. The Turin Show, however, opened midway through the London Motor Show, and it was this which confused the media at the time. Unfortunately, British Leyland's press office seems to have done nothing to explain what was going on. It also failed to explain why the new Spitfire carried Roman numerals (Mk IV) when earlier versions of the car had displayed their designations in Arabic (Mk 2 and Mk 3). In retrospect, however, it seems probable that Triumph wanted to avoid confusion with the original Spitfire 4.

The most obvious differences between Mk 3 and Mk IV Spitfires were in the styling, which had been revitalized to give the car a closer family resemblance to the new Stag grand tourer which had been announced in June. Triumph had once again sought the assistance of Michelotti in the restyling, but had rejected the Italian's initial proposal for a streamlined front end with pop-up headlamps. At the time most motor manufacturers viewed the American legislators as resembling loose cannons, and Triumph was afraid that they might outlaw such headlamps on cars sold in the USA. The pop-up lamps would also have been relatively costly to manufacture, might have given trouble in service and would have brought about the demise of the Spitfire's much-liked, forward-hinged front end.

And so the front end was simply tidied up. The weld seams along the wing tops disappeared, the chromed headlamp surrounds were changed for painted ones and a new, black, plastic grille was fitted. The wheelarches were flared slightly (mainly to allow for wider tyres on the GT6, which shared the same pressings), and a narrower bumper was fitted. This wrapped around the sides to integrate better with the styling than it had on the Mk 3 and was fitted with large, black, plastic under-riders.

The rest of the Michelotti makeover has

The prototype Spitfire Mk IVs

Two Spitfire Mk IV engineering prototypes are recorded, with the experimental Commission Numbers X793 and X800.

X793 was a left-hand drive car and was registered as RVC 436 H, in the number sequence which also embraced the press-launch Stags. It was probably built in late 1969 or early 1970. Triumph records describe it as the first engine prototype, with the engine number FE 36140, and note that it had Kangol seat belts.

X800 had right-hand drive and was built in May 1970. It was later registered as TKV 38 J. The car was painted white and was the second engine prototype, with the engine number X 1220 E. It was fitted (probably later) with an 'S-4' engine (probably Spitfire Mk IV rather than slant-four) and with 1975 model-year bumpers.

The Mk IV looked even better from behind, with the latest Triumph corporate tail styling and new plate badges on the rear wings. This car is in fact Engineering prototype number X793. Despite the British registration number, it has American-market features, with side marker lights and high-back seats.

The new rear end styling was derived from that of the Stag, although it actually appeared first on the second-generation Triumph 2000 saloon range. The original concept dated back to 1965 and Michelotti's first prototype for the Stag.

Although the front bumper height remained as it had been on the Mk 3, this time the bumper blade was much better integrated into the overall styling.

Plate badging on the bonnet tied in with the general style of badging which was by this time in use on all British Leyland cars. The large rubber overriders were not intended to meet Federal laws; there were special ones for the USA.

Identification and production: Spitfire Mk IV

The Commission Number of a Spitfire Mk IV is in the same place as on earlier models. The numbering sequence is: FH 3 to FH 64995, and within the same sequence, Federal-specification models for the USA have an FK prefix, Swedish-market cars have an FL prefix and the 1500-engined cars for the USA have an FM prefix.

In theory, therefore, there were 64,993 Mk IV models, including the 1500s for the USA. However, once again it is not possible to tie these figures up with annual production figures which are organized by calendar year. Other sources quote Mk IV production as 70,021.

Spitfire Mk IV engines have numbers prefixed by FH, by FK (US models), or by FL (Swedish models, from 1971). Gearboxes and final drives have the same FH prefix. However, the 1500 engines for the USA carry an FM prefix.

---

sometimes been described as a re-skin of the Spitfire, which is a reasonable description. However, the only outer panels to remain unchanged were the body sills and the doors. Even the doors had new flush-fitting handles and they now had different drop-glasses with squared-off top edges instead of the round type on earlier cars. The windscreen was now no longer removable for competition. Instead, its frame was now integral with the scuttle top panel, which provided the rigidity for the glass area to be increased in depth by 2in – a feature welcomed by tall drivers.

The rear wings and the tail were completely altered. Although the welded rib-type seams along the tops of the rear wings were still present, they had been de-emphasized by the removal of their chromed cappings, and the rear end had been squared off with a recessed, vertical tail panel with a chromed surround like that pioneered on the Stag. New light clusters now incorporated the reversing lights for the first time and the number-plate lights were fitted in the bumper, in a Stag-like plinth which bore a Triumph nameplate. The whole rear of the car looked much tidier and more modern than before, and the restyling had the additional benefit of increasing the space in the boot

by a small amount.

Also contributing to the more modern look were restyled road wheels, with radial brake cooling slots and a black polycarbonate 'hub cap' which carried the Spitfire name on its central medallion. As for the badges, there were novelties here too. The bonnet now bore only a plate badge reading 'Spitfire IV', and there was no badge on the vertical tail panel. Instead, there was a 'Spitfire IV' plate badge on the side of each rear wing. The front wings also carried small, rectangular plate badges with the British Leyland name and encircled L logo.

There were major changes inside too. The redesigned dashboard introduced on the 1969-model American Federal Mk 3s was now standardized for all markets, at long last putting the instruments in front of the driver where he could actually see them. The new facia was covered in the same black leathercloth as on American Mk 3s, but featured new flush switchgear to meet safety regulations, and there were new plain door trims with recessed handles. Restyled seats, essentially the same as those introduced on the 1969 Federal Mk 3s but without the large fixed head restraints, were part of the package, and sun visors, safety belts and a heater were all standard equipment. Non-overdrive

The matt black dashboard at last put the main dials directly in front of the driver; 1973 and later Mk IVs had a wood-veneered facia of essentially similar design. Note the shield badge on the steering wheel boss, which would give way to a simple Triumph name when the new dash was introduced. This car is equipped with an overdrive and the sliding control switch can be seen in the gear-lever knob.

The soft top was also restyled for the Mk IV, as this example shows. The rear wing badges are missing from this car.

Although Mk IV models still had the 1,296cc engine, the under-bonnet view differed. One of the new half-height engine valances can be seen in the foreground, while in the background one of the two sections of black air intake trunking which led to the air cleaner is visible.

cars had a reshaped gear-lever knob, and when overdrive was fitted there was now a new knob with a sliding switch to engage and disengage the overdrive. The pedals, too, were different, and those for the brake and the clutch now carried British Leyland's encircled L symbol moulded into their rubber pads.

There were changes to both the hardtop and the soft top as well. The hardtop had been restyled with a flatter roof to suit the squared-off tail styling and now sported new opening rear quarter-lights. It was the work of Triumph's own stylists rather than

of Michelotti. As for the soft top, it had been recontoured to suit the squared-off tops to the door glasses, while the hood frame inside was now shielded by plastic mouldings, which were presumably intended to lessen injuries to the occupants in the event of a collison.

Under the bonnet, the first things to catch an observer's eye were the new half-height engine valances, with a cut-out on the right-hand one which served no purpose except on American-market cars, when it fitted around the air cleaner for the single carburettor. The new seven-bladed,

---

Performance figures: Spitfire Mk IV

The 1971-model Spitfire Mk IV had a top speed of 97mph (155km/h) and could reach 60mph from rest in around 12.5 sec. However, the lower-revving, 61bhp engine fitted on 1972 and later models brought with it poorer performance. Top speed with this engine dropped to 95mph (152km/h) and the 0–60mph time went up by a massive two seconds to 14.5. Fuel consumption with either engine was around 35mpg (8.1l/100km).

The Federal 1500-engined version of the Spitfire Mk IV had very similar performance figures to the later Federal Spitfire 1500 (see Chapter 8).

---

orange, plastic fan, introduced to cut down noise, would also have caught the attention, and the black trunking which now ducted cold air into the air cleaner was an obvious change. Most of the other changes were invisible though.

The engine itself was still in essence the same 1,296cc unit which had been so successful in the Mk 3 models, now fitted with the con-rods and larger big-end bearings of the six-cylinder engines in order to simplify parts manufacture and storage. The crankcase breathing system had been modified yet again, and the large disc-like PVC valve was no longer in evidence. A cable accelerator linkage was a welcome improvement, and there was now also an alternator in place of the dynamo. A redesigned exhaust system was now fitted; this no longer had a central expansion box but instead had an additional transverse silencer at the rear, just ahead of the bumper – an arrangement pioneered on the GT6 Mk 2 in 1968. Triumph quoted the power output of the Mk IV engine as 63bhp, which led many to conclude that it had been detuned from the Mk 3 engine which had boasted 75bhp. That was not, in fact, the case: what had happened was that the motor industry had switched over to a new and stricter system of rating engine output – the German DIN system – which now gave the figures with the ancillaries installed. The 1,296cc engine was just as

powerful as before, and it was not this which made the Spitfire Mk IV slower off the mark than the Mk 3 had been.

The loss of acceleration was brought about by three factors, and when these are considered it is surprising that the car was not even less accelerative. The first was that it had put on weight as compared with its predecessor. The second was that it now had taller final drive gearing of 3.89:1 as against 4.11:1, a change brought about mainly to improve fuel economy and to provide more restful high-speed cruising. And the third factor was that the Mk IV had a new gearbox, with a taller 3.5:1 first gear in place of the earlier 3.75:1. This gearbox was carried within a casing which closely resembled that of the GT6 and the Vitesse, but was slightly longer, and its most important feature was that it brought synchromesh on bottom gear to the Spitfire at long last. Developed for the Triumph Toledo saloon, it would also appear later in other British Leyland cars.

The rear suspension had been re-engineered, as well. The GT6-style set-up with its double-jointed drive-shafts would have been an obvious choice for the Spitfire, but it had been ruled out on cost grounds. Instead, Triumph had developed a simpler system which was nearly as effective and was known as the 'swing-spring' set-up. The engineers had known for some time that most of the Spitfire's handling problems had been caused by excessive roll

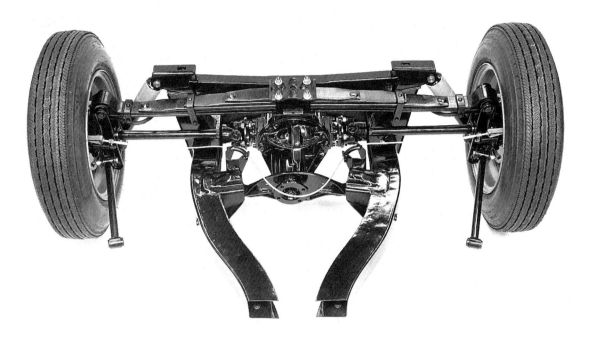

The 'swing-spring' suspension of the Mk IV Spitfire brought some welcome handling improvements.

stiffness in the transverse rear spring; but they also knew that simply to reduce the stiffness of the spring would allow the car to drag its tail when fully laden. Therefore they devised a layout which retained the full spring stiffness to counter vertical bumps, but which reduced that stiffness when the car was cornering.

In place of the six leaves of the earlier rear spring there were just five, and the topmost of these was clamped firmly to the differential, as before. However, the other four were mounted on a round pin in the centre of the clamp and were free to pivot slightly around this. Thus, when cornering, the spring leaves shifted slightly and did not contribute to suspension stiffness, which was all handled by the single main leaf and by a beefed-up anti-roll bar. To balance the handling, there was also a fatter anti-roll bar on the front axle.

WHAT THE BRITISH PRESS THOUGHT

When *Autosport* magazine reported on the new Spitfire Mk IV in its issue of 29 October 1970, the test staff had been lucky enough to take the car round the Silverstone circuit to see how it behaved at high speeds. On the whole, the latest rear suspension was very successful:

> The Spitfire is now very well-behaved, even when driven harder than would previously have been advisable. With very little roll, it fairly flies through the bends and handles far better than its predecessor. As a sports car it is greatly improved, but the suspension gives a hard ride.

However, the taller axle gearing did mean that the car was now greatly over-geared in

These days generally known as a Mk 1, the original Spitfire 4 was always a very pretty car. This well-preserved 1963 example is original in almost every respect.

(Above) *The Spitfire was always strictly a two-seater car. Note the piping around the seats on this 1963 model. The steering wheel is a later addition: the original would have been a black plastic type with two spokes.*

(Left) *The big, front-hinged bonnet made servicing a simple matter. This is the 1,147cc engine of a Spitfire 4. Early cars like this had no engine side valances.*

(Below) *Wedgwood Blue paint sets off this Mk 2 Spitfire to perfection. From this angle, differences from the original Spitfire 4 were hard to spot . . .*

. . . but the new vinyl covering for the dashboard was immediately apparent from a look inside. The steering wheel on this car was an approved accessory.

The raised front bumper gave the Mk 3 Spitfire a distinctive appearance, although the car lost none of its prettiness. This is a 1968 car; from 1970, the windscreen pillars were blacked out.

Rear bumpers were raised on the Mk 3, too, which now boasted reversing lights as standard.

The Spitfire Mk IV and 1500 shared less curvaceous body styling, which was handsome rather than pretty. This is a late-model 1500.

The squared-off rear end of the 1500 gave the car a more modern appearance.

(Above) *From 1977, Spitfire interiors featured houndstooth-check wearing surfaces on the seats. This very late 1500 has the final style of black, three-spoke steering wheel.*

(Top right and below) *The GT6 had a personality all of its own, and its availability as a closed car only reinforced this. Nevertheless, the family resemblance to the contemporary Spitfire was obvious. This is a 1969 GT6 Mk 1.*

The key to the GT6's character was its 2-litre engine.

A wooden dashboard added to the appeal of the GT6 Mk 1.

This GT6 Mk 2 once saw service with the Dorset Police. Note the Rostyle wheel trims, the bonnet louvres and the louvres behind the side windows – all changes introduced for the Mk 2.

The final iteration of the GT6 was the Mk 3, which shared the squarer lines introduced on the Mk IV Spitfire. To some eyes, this was the most attractive GT6 of them all.

In Britain, the aftermarket specialists Lenham manufactured three different hardtops for the Mk IV Spitfire, and these could also be fitted to the later 1500 models. The Easyfitting top is shown here with a black colour bonded leathergrain finish and was similar to the factory hardtop but lacked its rear side window...

...the Fastback top in this picture was painted to match the car ...

... and the Torado seen here normally had a leathergrain top panel while the rear section was painted to match the body. Like the TR4 'Surrey' top, which obviously inspired it, the Torado could be supplied with a folding fabric roof section as well.

overdrive top. This reduced the value of the overdrive, although it was still useful for quick gearshifts when sprinting from corner to corner on a fast road.

The *Autocar* staff were also full of praise for the improved suspension. 'It seems almost impossible now to get the back wheels to tuck under, and flick the car into a potentially frightening oversteer situation', they concluded in the road test published on 11 March 1971. The higher gearing had reduced the car's accelerative ability, but had also made it much quieter and had led to an impressive improvement in fuel economy. *Autocar* considered that the Spitfire Mk IV had 'lost virtually all the vices of the previous car'.

Even so, there were still disappointing elements. The new seats offered poor lateral location, and the dead-feeling brakes

The creation of Rover-Triumph

British Leyland – properly the British Leyland Motor Corporation – was formed in 1968 by the merger of the Leyland group of companies and British Motor Holdings. It brought together under a single umbrella all three of Britain's principal sports car manufacturers: MG, Jaguar and Triumph. All had well-established model ranges, and so the BL management allowed them to carry on undisturbed for the first two years of the new corporation's existence. However, once it became time to think of new models, the management quite sensibly saw an opportunity to rationalize its model ranges in the interests of greater cost-effectiveness.

Equally sensibly, although it may have been heartbreaking for fans of the several marques, BL set about rationalizing its engineering staffs in the early 1970s. The reasons behind all the changes made are too numerous and complicated to explain here, but the effect on Triumph was to split the company asunder. Although assembly remained at Canley and at the Speke factory in Liverpool, the Triumph engineering department was merged with Rover's and its styling department moved to Longbridge, traditional home of Austin. Under the Rover-Triumph name a completely new product strategy was drawn up for the 1970s. Among the cars it encompassed were the Triumph TR7 and the TR8, both sharing a number of major mechanical components with the big, new Rover SD1 saloon.

Despite these brave new plans, British Leyland did not intend to sweep away existing money-making products until absolutely necessary. And so the Spitfire was kept in production. But it was as a result of the new 'corporate engineering' plans introduced at this time that both the Spitfire and its long-standing MG Midget rival would eventually be fitted with the same 1,493cc Triumph engine.

Dealer accessories: Spitfire Mk IV

There were far fewer accessories offered for the Mk IV than for previous cars, mainly because so much more was now standard equipment on the latest model.

Continental touring kit
Hardtop
Headlamp conversion mask for continental touring (by Lucas)
Hood stowage cover (for use with hardtop)
Mud flaps (rear wheels only)
Oil cooler
Radio (including speaker and aerial)
Skid plate
Soft-top conversion kit (for cars supplied new with hardtop only)
Touch-in paints
Towbar
Wire wheels (bolt-on type; up to FH 60000 only)
Wooden gear knob

needed a hard shove on the pedal and did not resist fade too well. Nevertheless, scuttle shake was reduced, the interior layout was 'much more logical', and this latest version of the model was 'a fast, good handling sports car which now looks so much more refined than its predecessors.'

PRODUCTION CHANGES TO THE MK IV SPITFIRE

Relatively few important production changes were made to the Spitfire Mk IV, although detailed modifications were made more or less continuously, as was Triumph practice. The biggest changes were introduced all together in February 1973, with effect from Commission Number FH 50000.

There were some important engine changes, however, introduced at Commission Number FH 25000. Mainly to reduce manufacturing costs, the Toledo saloon type of cylinder head was fitted, with its bigger inlet valves and slightly different porting. At the same time, a less sporty camshaft was fitted, in this case intended to reduce exhaust emissions and fuel consumption. This now ran directly in the block, which was modified to suit, and dispensed with the separate bearings of earlier engines. The overall result of these

A tonneau cover was standard from 1974. It was also possible to order a tonneau cover without the special pouches for cars without headrests, although there was always a shaped section for the steering wheel.

Factory-installed options: Spitfire Mk IV

Competition brake pads (Ferodo DS 11)
Grease nipples on front upper ball joint, rear bearing housing and vertical link
Head restraints (from FH 60000)
Leather upholstery (to FH 50000 only)
Overdrive
Radial tyres, 145 SR 13 type (to FH 38271 only)
Tonneau cover (standard from 1974)
Toughened glass windscreen ('Zebra-Zone' type)
Whitewall tyres

---

changes was to reduce the power to 61bhp at 5,500rpm, from 63bhp at 6,000rpm, and to reduce the torque to 68lb.ft at 2,900rpm from 69.8lb.ft at 3,500rpm. This made little difference to the acceleration, but it did reduce the maximum speed to around 95 from the 97mph (to 152 from 155km/h) of which the first Mk IVs were capable.

There were two other changes of note before the February 1973 watershed. The first, chronologically, was that the original stainless-steel windscreen finisher was changed to a cheaper, bright, plastic type. Although this type of penny-pinching was typical of British Leyand's influence, Triumph's masters should perhaps not be blamed for this, as a similar change had been made early in Spitfire Mk 1 production, long before the British Leyland days. The second change was a more important one, to wider 155 SR 13 tyres in place of the 145 SR 13s of the early Mk IVs. This further improved the car's roadholding.

The February 1973 changes represented a major facelift for the Spitfire and were probably intended to maintain its appeal in the face of increased competition, especially in the USA. Most of the changes affected the interior, but a smaller 7.25gal (33l) fuel tank replaced the earlier 8.25gal (37.5l) type (for unexplained reasons), and a stronger Laycock J-type overdrive replaced the earlier D-type, mainly to increase commonality with other Triumph cars of the

The later Mk IV models could be easily recognized by a black under-bumper air dam, just visible in this picture.

time. With it came a slightly taller gearing of 0.797:1 in place of the earlier 0.802:1. The rear track was also widened by 2in through the use of longer drive-shafts, which had the beneficial effect of increasing the wheels' negative camber. The rear wheels of these later Spitfires thus had a pronounced lean inwards at the top, but it was all to the good as far as handling was concerned.

The predominant feature of the new interior was a wood-veneered dashboard in place of the black vinyl type. The layout remained unchanged, but there were also new and clearer instrument dials. The steering wheel was changed yet again and the new one had a 14.5in (368mm) diameter instead of the 15in (381mm) of the old; it also had a new horn push with fake stitching moulded around its edges and the

Triumph name in the centre instead of the old Triumph shield. Reclining seats with optional, detachable head restraints were a further improvement, and, in the excitement which all these changes created, few people noticed that white soft tops had been withdrawn; from now on black was the only colour option.

There were a few more changes before production of the Mk IV models ended in November 1974. The major modifications made to American-market models are covered separately, but cars for the rest of the world were modified at FH 60000, with a black chin spoiler at the front. At the same time, there was further manufacturing rationalization as the inlet manifold was changed for the type found on other 1,296cc Triumphs of the time.

Triumph Spitfire Mk IV (1970–74)

Layout
All-steel bodyshell bolted to steel backbone-frame chassis; two-seater open sports car, with front engine and rear-wheel drive.

Engine

Block material	cast iron
Head material	cast iron
Cylinders	four, in line
Cooling	water
Bore and stroke	73.7mm × 76mm (2.90in × 2.99in)
	1973 US models: 73.7mm 87.5mm (2.90in × 3.44in)
Capacity	1,296cc (79.1 cu.in)
	1973 US models: 1,493cc (91.1 cu.in)
Valves	overhead, two per cylinder
Compression ratio	9.0:1
	1972 US models: 8.0:1
	1973 US models: 7.5:1
Carburettors	two SU type HS2E (1.25in)
	1971–72 US models: single Zenith-Stromberg
	1973 US models: two SU
Max. power	63bhp at 6,000rpm (61bhp at 5,500rpm from FH 25000)
	1971 US models: 58bhp at 5,200rpm
	1972 US models: 48bhp at 5,500rpm

Max. torque	1973 models: 57bhp at 5,000rpm
	69.8lb.ft at 3,500rpm (68lb.ft at 2,900rpm from FH 25000)
	1971 US models: 72lb.ft at 3,000rpm
	1972 US models: 69 lb.ft at 2900rpm
	1973 US models: 74 lb.ft at 3000rpm

Transmission

Hydraulically-operated diaphragm clutch with 6.5in diameter; four-speed all-synchromesh manual gearbox with optional overdrive (Laycock D-type or, from FH 60000, Laycock J-type).

Gearbox ratios

Top	1.00:1
Third	1.39:1
Second	2.16:1
First	3.50:1
Reverse	3.99:1
Overdrive	0.802:1 (D-type) or 0.797:1 (J-type)
Final drive ratio	3.89:1
	1972 US models: 4.11:1

Suspension and steering

Front	independent, with twin wishbones, coil springs, anti-roll bar and telescopic dampers
Rear	independent, with swing-axles, radius arms, transverse leaf spring and telescopic dampers
Steering	rack and pinion, with 3.75:1 ratio
Tyres	5.20×13 crossply; 155 SR 13 radials standard from FH 38271
Wheels	four-stud, steel type standard
	centre-lock wire type optional
Rim width	4.5in

Brakes

Type	discs at the front
	drums at the rear
Size	disc diameter 9in
	drum diameter 7in, width 1.25in

Dimensions [in(mm)]

Wheelbase	83(2,108)
Track, front	49(1,245)
Track, rear	48(1,220); 50(1,270) from FH 50000 (1972 model-year)
Overall length	149(3,785)
Overall width	58.5(1,486)
Overall height	47.5(1,206)
Unladen weight	1,717lb/779kg

Paint and trim colours: Spitfire Mk IV

All cars had the code numbers of their original body and trim colours stamped on to their Commission Number plates. In some cases the same code number was used for both the body and the trim colour.

January – December 1971
There were nine exterior colours, of which eight were carried over from the final Spitfire Mk 3 and the GT6 Mk 2 range; the new colour was Sapphire Blue, which replaced Royal Blue. Five interior colours were available, of which four were carried over from the previous models; the new option was Silver Grey. The combinations available were:

Body colour	Upholstery colour
Damson Red	black, Silver Grey or tan
Laurel Green	black, Matador Red or tan
Saffron Yellow	black or tan
Sapphire Blue	Silver Grey or Shadow Blue
Sienna Brown	black or tan
Signal Red	black or tan
Valencia Blue	black or tan
Wedgwood Blue	black or Shadow Blue
White	black, Matador Red, Shadow Blue or tan

January – August 1972
The range was reduced to seven, of which five were retained from the previous options list; the newcomers were Emerald Green and Pimento Red; Laurel Green, Signal Red, Valencia Blue and Wedgwood Blue were dropped. There were now four trim colours instead of five; Matador Red had been dropped but the other four were as before. The options were:

Body colour	Upholstery colour
Damson Red	black, Silver Grey or tan
Emerald Green	black or Silver Grey
Pimento Red	black
Saffron Yellow	black
Sapphire Blue	black, Shadow Blue or Silver Grey
Sienna Brown	tan
White	black, Shadow Blue or tan

September 1972 – January 1973
The range was increased to eight, as Damson Red and Saffron Yellow were dropped, and carmine Red, French Blue and Mallard Green were added. There were again four trim options, Chestnut being a new colour in place of Silver Grey. The choices available were:

Body colour	Upholstery colour
Carmine Red	black or tan
Emerald Green	black
French Blue	black
Mallard Green	black or tan
Pimento Red	black or Chestnut

Sapphire Blue   black or Shadow Blue
Sienna Brown   black or tan
White   black, Shadow Blue or Chestnut

February 1973 – September 1974
The range was increased again, this time to ten colours, and all eight of the previous season's offerings remained available. Magenta and Mimosa Yellow were the new ones. The same four trim options remained available. The choices were:

Body colour	Upholstery colour
Carmine Red	black or tan
Emerald Green	black
French Blue	black
Magenta	black
Mallard Green	black or tan
Mimosa Yellow	black or Chestnut
Pimento Red	black or Chestnut
Sapphire Blue	black or Shadow Blue
Sienna Brown	black or tan
White	black, Shadow Blue or Chestnut

THE FEDERAL SPITFIRE MK IV

It was in this period that American Federal regulations began to bite hard. The first Federal Mk IV Spitfires had the single-Stromberg 1,296cc engine with 68bhp; but to meet the 1971 model-year standards Triumph had to detune that by a massive 10bhp, so that it put out 58bhp while twin-SU models for the rest of the world were still rated at 71bhp. In the much heavier Mk IV the difference really showed. And there was worse to come. For 1972 further detuning was necessary, and this time engine output dropped to a miserable 48bhp while the compression ratio went down to 8.0:1 from the previous season's 9.0:1. Torque plummeted to 61lb.ft. Triumph did its best to compensate by fitting a lower final-drive ratio of 4.11:1 in place of the 3.89:1 still standard in other markets, but a 1972 Federal Mk IV was no match for an early 1,147cc Spitfire on acceleration or top speed. Thus it was no real surprise when the 1973 models were fitted with a new and more powerful engine which would not become available in Spitfires sold elsewhere until the end of 1974.

This new engine was a long-stroke derivative of the existing 1,296cc type, with a displacement of 1,493cc. New to the Spitfire, it was nevertheless not new to Triumph because it had entered production in 1970 for the front-wheel-drive 1500 saloon. Slightly earlier than that, production had started in South Africa for locally-assembled Triumph saloons, and the engine's origins could be traced back at least as far as 1966 when a prototype 1.5-litre engine was tested in a Spitfire. When fitted with a single Stromberg 150 CDSE carburettor and appropriate emission-control equipment for the American market, it gave 57bhp at 5,000rpm and 73lb.ft at 3,000rpm, figures which were much more healthy than those for the final 1,296cc

Federal engines. *Road and Track* tested one to 94mph (150km/h) in May 1973, and saw 60mph (100km/h) come up in 15.4 sec, all on the tall 3.89:1 axle ratio. This performance was no advance on pre-emission-control days, but at least it was not a further step backwards.

The 1973 and the 1974 Federal Spitfires with this new engine were known – and badged – as Spitfire 1500s. Strictly speaking, therefore, they were no longer Mk IV models, although they had none of the other changes which came in with the Spitfire 1500 introduced for all other mar-

kets at the end of 1974 and sold in the USA as a 1975 model. That car was also easily distinguishable from the original Federal Spitfire 1500 by its decal badges; the 1973 and 1974 models had metal badges of the same design as those on the Spitfire Mk IV.

There were other special features about the Federal Spitfires which tend to pale into insignificance alongside the story of their chronic losses of power and performance. Narrow-band, whitewall tyres were still standard and all cars had side marker lamps and the high-back seats with fixed

Not the prettiest of Spitfires, this is a 1974 American-specification 1500 model. Essentially a re-engined Mk IV, it also sports the impact-resistant over-riders which American models had to have at this time.

head restraints. In addition, it appears that most, and possibly all, Federal Mk IV models had a contrasting side-stripe decal which ran along each flank at door-handle height.

WHAT THE AMERICAN PRESS SAID

Not many reviews of the 1,296cc Mk IV were published in the USA. *Road Test* spent two weeks with an early 68bhp example and published a report in its July 1971 issue. But that would be the last road test published in a major American magazine before the 1500 model arrived for 1973: British Leyland was none too keen for any publicity about what emissions controls were doing to the cars. The *Road Test* staff regretted that their car was supplied without the optional overdrive. They welcomed the arrival of synchromesh on first gear, mainly because the car would not pull well in second at 10mph (15km/h) and below. The steering needed too many turns from lock to lock, and 'the ride is harsher than most of its kind at low speeds'. Yet it was still an enjoyable small sports car: 'It may not actually go very fast, or get up to cruising speeds with more than acceptable alacrity, but it *feels* like it does.'

As far as the 'Mk IV' Spitfire 1500 was concerned, Triumph had undoubtedly got the mixture right, however. In *Car and Driver's* 1974 annual poll readers voted the new model top of the sports/GT category, which was a tremendous accolade for a design now twelve years old. And in that May 1973 road test already mentioned, *Road and Track* added praise for the new engine to its enthusiasm for the latest handling improvements. It thought that it 'doesn't have the 'brute' acceleration of the pre-emission 1,296 engine but it more than makes up for a lack of power by a welcome increase in torque in the low- and middle-rpm range.'

7 GT6 Mk 3 (1970–73)

The GT6 Mk 2 and its Federal equivalent the GT6+ had been so well received that it might look at first glance as if there was no need for a further revised version of Triumph's small sports coupé. However, sales of the GT6 had been slipping since 1968, and to have left the model with its earlier styling when the Spitfire was being updated as a Mk IV with smart new skin panels would have been tantamount to commercial suicide. So the GT6 Mk 3 was created as a companion model to the Spitfire Mk IV.

From almost every point of view it was

The new styling suited the GT6 very well indeed, giving it a sleeker and more purposeful look than before. This early car was pictured at the Silverstone racing circuit.

Paint and trim colours: GT6 Mk 3

The GT6 Mk 3 was available in the same range of paints and trims as the contemporary Spitfire Mk IV. For details see the tables in Chapter 6. GT6 production, of course, finished before that of the Spitfire Mk IV, so the final combinations were available only between February and November 1973. During this period the GT6 had brushed nylon upholstery in the same range of colours as the vinyl used on the Spitfire Mk IV.

---

arguably the best version of the model to be made. Inexplicably, however, the improvements it incorporated failed to reverse the sales slide. The biggest problem was almost certainly the huge power losses which the car suffered in the USA for the 1972 season, when brake horsepower was reduced to little more than that of a home-market Spitfire. A final attempt to stem the tide for the 1973 season was a complete failure, and sales dropped by about 42 per cent – whereas the 1972 figures had only been about 9 per cent down on those for 1971. Triumph enthusiasts tend to clutch at straws when trying to explain the GT6's early demise, suggesting that the British Leyland management favoured the rival MGB GT, but the plain fact was that the GT6 was not selling. Just 2,745 of them were sold world-wide in the 1973 season, and British Leyland was in no financial position to keep such lame ducks alive. Production was therefore halted in November that year.

Like the Spitfire Mk IV, the GT6 Mk 3 was announced to the world at the Turin Motor Show in October 1970 and did not become available through the showrooms until the beginning of 1971. From the start there was no doubting the success of the re-skin, which probably suited the GT6 even better than it did the Spitfire.

Starting at the front, it shared the new bonnet styling with the slimmer and better-integrated front bumper, although the six-cylinder car still had a power bulge in the

bonnet which was not on the four-cylinder model. Even that was new, though; it was wider and flatter than the bulge on the earlier GT6s and gave a much smoother and less 'modified' appearance. The Mk 3 GT6

The reflection in this bonnet panel makes clear that the picture was taken at a Triumph enthusiasts' gathering on a sunny day. Visible here are the optional bonnet lock and the British Leyland logo applied to some cars.

Recessed door handles with chromed escutcheons were an important part of the styling update on these cars.

bonnet also dispensed with the four sets of louvres which had distinguished the Mk 2 type. To complete the transformation, it carried a new, corporate-style black and chrome 'GT6 Mk 3' badge and there were British Leyland badges behind the wheelarches.

The Mk 3 GT6 had the same deeper windscreen as the Spitfire Mk IV, which was optionally available in laminated glass and with the green-tinted Sundym heat-resistant glass which could be specified at extra cost for the whole of the passenger cabin. The door handles were the same flush-fitting, chromed type and the sills had the bright finisher which had been introduced on the Mk 2 GT6. From the door shut pillars backwards, however, there were many changes.

First of all, the rearmost side windows had been reprofiled at their trailing edges to give a less awkward shape. Behind them were new and longer ventilation louvres, now painted in the body colour rather than chromed as on the Mk 2. The left-hand rear wing also carried the fuel filler – repositioned from the tail and accompanied by a different fuel tank. The filler cap was a lockable, flush-fitting, chromed type like that fitted to the Stag and the 2000 Estate. At the rear, the GT6 now had Spitfire Mk IV-type styling, with the fastback blended neatly into a short, flat, rear deck. The tailgate catch had been redesigned and its release was now similar to that on the Spitfire Mk IV and the heated rear window now had horizontal heating elements (although some early cars used old-stock

The biggest success was at the rear, however, where the new corporate tail styling and the modified rear roofline gave the car a much more modern appearance. Note that there is chrome around the tail panel, but that the join between wing and body is covered in a matt black finisher.

Nose badging left no doubt about the car's identity.

Under the bonnet of a Mk 3 GT6, showing the silver-painted rocker cover and the large emissions-control valve towards the rear of the engine.

Mk 2 types with their vertical elements).

Little had changed under the bonnet, although the carburettors were now emission-controlled, Zenith-Stromberg 150CDSE models, operated for the first time by a cable linkage. As on the Spitfire Mk IV, there was also a brightly-coloured, plastic, cooling fan, and black trunking fed air from alongside the radiator to the carburettor air box. In practice, the engine was in exactly the same state of tune as in the Mk 2 cars, but paper figures made it appear detuned: the Mk 3 engine figures were given as 98bhp at 5,300rpm and 108lb.ft at 3,000rpm, as compared with 104bhp and 117.3lb.ft at the same crankshaft speeds. Even some otherwise knowledgeable writers have been caught out by this, which simply reflected British Leyland's use of stricter DIN standards and the same change on the Spitfire.

There was also a change to the exhaust system, which now sported a centre silencer once again in addition to the transverse rear silencer introduced on the GT6 Mk 2. This rear silencer was not the same as on the earlier car, however: distinguished by its angled, twin tailpipes, it was actually acoustically tuned and, in conjunction with the new centre box, gave a pleasingly deep exhaust note to the Mk 3 models. The transmission remained unchanged from the Mk 2 cars, except that the 3.89:1 final drive was reinstated as standard for overdrive-equipped cars outside the USA. The road wheels still had 4.5in rims, but Triumph had abandoned the cheap-looking wheel covers of the Mk 2 in favour of the pressed-steel pattern used on the Spitfire Mk IV. These carried chromed rather than black centre panels and, uniquely, they had centre caps bearing the GT6 name. Wire wheels remained available at extra cost, but they were no longer the traditional 'knock-off' splined type; instead, they bolted to the standard hubs.

Finally, there were interior changes, too. The dashboard had flush switchgear like the Spitfire Mk IV, plus modified heater controls. The overdrive switch was now found in the gear lever knob – again as on the Spitfire Mk IV – and there were restyled door trims with flush-fitting handles. For most markets there was also a new ignition keylock which incorporated a steering lock and was mounted rather awkwardly underneath the parcels shelf.

The GT6 Mk 3 prototypes

There were just two engineering prototypes of the GT6 Mk 3. These were numbered as X 797 and X799.

X797 was a right-hand-drive car and was registered as PHP 439 H. It is described in the records of Triumph's experimental cars as the first engine prototype, and had the engine number X1257 E.

X799 had left-hand drive and was a white car which was probably never registered. It had the engine number KD 78921 E and is described in the records as the '2nd eng. prototype'. It is not clear in this case whether 'eng.' stood for engine or engineering. The car was crashed and scrapped.

Plans for the face-lift which would create the Mk IV Spitfire and the Mk 3 GT6 were being made as early as 1968. Triumph's stylists were keen on this design, grafted on to a GT6 for viewing purposes. Note the British Leyland corporate badge on the nose and the alternative versions of the bonnet presented for viewing. On the side nearer the camera there is no central hump and the louvres are incorporated as a feature behind the headlamp cover. On the far side, the louvres are at the back of the bonnet and there is a central hump. The headlamps would have been raised electrically.

Eyeball air vents and new rocker switches characterized the GT6 Mk 3 dashboard, which also had a curiously-positioned ignition keylock, just visible here between the gear lever and the dashboard.

Factory-installed options: GT6 Mk 3

Grease nipples for front upper ball joints
Grease nipples for track rod ends
Laminated windscreen
Leather trim panels (to KE 20000 only)
Leather upholstery
Overdrive
Skid plate
Sundym tinted glass (standard from KE 20001)

Dealer accessories: GT6 Mk 3

Brake servo (Girling Powerstop type; standard from KE 20001)
Continental touring kit
Headlamp converter masks (Lucas)
Head restraints (from KE20001 only)
Luggage straps
Occasional rear seat
Oil cooler
Radio with speaker and aerial
Sunroof (Tudor Webasto folding type; fitted by specialists)
Tow bar
Wire wheels (bolt-on type)
Wooden gear knob

PRODUCTION CHANGES TO THE GT6 MK 3

Every penny of the budget Triumph could allocate to the GT6 in the early 1970s went on keeping the car saleable in the USA. To ensure that the engine met ever-tightening exhaust-emissions regulations and that the car as a whole met increasingly stringent safety standards was not a cheap process. So between 1970 and 1972 the GT6 did not change in any significant respect outside the USA. As on the Spitfire Mk IV, the original stainless-steel windscreen finisher was soon replaced by a cheaper, bright, plastic type. It also looks as if the fitting of the British Leyland badge on the front wings was not as consistent as it might have been, and later cars had their GT6 wheel-centre caps replaced by caps bearing the encircled-L symbol.

Then from car number KE 10001, at the beginning of 1972, the engine was heavily altered to suit manufacturing rationaliza-

---

Identification and production: GT6 Mk 3

The Commission Number of a GT6 Mk 3 is in the same place as on earlier models. The numbering sequences were:

KE 1 to KE 4596 (1971 models)
KE 10001 to KE 14816 (1972 models)
KE 20001 to KE 24218 (1973 models).

Within these sequences Federal-specification models for the USA have a KF prefix and Swedish-market cars have KG.

In theory, therefore, there were 13,630 Mk 3 GT6s. However, some Commission Numbers appear not to have been issued because the total production figure for the model is quoted as 13,042.

GT6 Mk 3 engines and gearboxes have numbers prefixed by KE and the final drives have KC prefixes for the 3.27:1 type and KD prefixes for the 3.89:1 type.

tion and to assist in meeting exhaust-emissions standards in the USA. Triumph fitted the cylinder head from the 2000 saloon, which had rather deeper combustion chambers than the GT6 Mk 2 type. Domed pistons brought the compression ratio back up, but the 9.0:1 which resulted was lower than the GT6 had enjoyed before. A milder camshaft was also used, to improve the fuel consumption and reduce exhaust emissions. The results were 95bhp at 5,200rpm (down from 98bhp at 5,300rpm) and 106 instead of 108lb.ft at 3,000rpm.

The GT6 remained unchanged for a further year, but in January 1973 it was substantially modified – just a month before a similar series of changes were made on the Spitfire Mk IV. Some of the modifications were the same as on the Spitfire, such as the addition of a black chin spoiler and the reinforcement of the front end of the chassis to improve the car's crashworthiness. But the main changes on the GT6 Mk 3 affected the rear suspension and the interior.

It was not that there was anything wrong with the existing rear suspension. Far from it, in fact, as the Rotoflex-jointed driveshafts and lower wishbones made the best of the transverse spring layout. What forced the change was that this suspension was relatively expensive to build and that after the Vitesse 2-litre went out of production in 1971 the GT6 Mk 3 was the only Triumph for which it was being made.

Whether Triumph would have gone down the same route without persuasion from British Leyland's accountants is a moot point, but a decision was taken to fit the GT6 with the cheaper 'swing-spring' suspension introduced on the Spitfire Mk IV. A stiffer transverse spring and bigger bushes were needed to suit the 2-litre car's higher performance and greater weight, but otherwise the installation was the same. Tyre pressures were also changed from those of the GT6 Mk

2. In everyday use the new suspension made no discernible difference to the handling, and it is doubtful whether many customers actually noticed the difference – or were told about it by showroom staff.

The interior changes were much more noticeable. For a start, the standard vinyl upholstery gave way to corded, brushed-nylon cloth on the wearing surfaces (although the sides and the backs of the seats were still covered in vinyl). This material was being introduced across the British Leyland range during this period and it offered excellent durability as well as much improved temperature control: vinyl could be both very cold in low temperatures and uncomfortably hot if exposed to sunlight for long periods. Temperature control of the GT6's interior was also improved by the standardization of the heat-resistant Sundym glass which had previously been an extra-cost option.

The new seats could also be fitted with head restraints at extra cost – not the ugly and bulky ones fitted to earlier Federal models but a neat, detachable type which did not obscure the view out of the back of the car. Other changes were to the dashboard, which normally had a rather darker wood veneer than before (although it appears that old stocks of the lighter type were also used up), and there were neater instrument faces with flush-fitting switchgear as well. The finishing touch was a TR6-type steering wheel, smaller than the earlier type and having flat, bare-metal spokes with stylish, elongated cut-outs.

Rather surprising this late in the day was the standardization of the brake servo which had earlier been an extra-cost option. With it came wider rear-brake drums and shoes, and the rear brake cylinders were changed to suit. Last but not least, the alternator on these final GT6s was a more powerful 16ACR type.

Triumph GT6 Mk 3 (1970–73)

Layout
All-steel bodyshell bolted to steel backbone-frame chassis; two-seater fastback coupé, with front engine and rear-wheel drive.

Engine

Block material	cast iron
Head material	cast iron
Cylinders	six, in line
Cooling	water
Bore and stroke	74.7mm × 76mm (2.94in × 2.99in)
Capacity	1,998cc (122 cu.in)
Valves	overhead, two per cylinder
Compression ratio	9.25:1 or 9.0:1 (from KC 10000)
	8.0:1 (1972 and 1973 models for USA)
Carburettors	two Zenith-Stromberg type 150 CDSE
Max. power	98bhp at 5,300rpm
	95bhp at 5,200rpm (from KC 10000)
	90bhp at 4,700rpm (1971 models for USA)
	79bhp at 4,900rpm (1972 and 1973 models for USA)
Max. torque	108lb.ft at 3,000rpm
	106lb.ft at 3,000rpm (from KC 10000)
	116lb.ft at 3,400rpm (1971 models for USA)
	97lb.ft at 2,900rpm (1972 and 1973 models for USA)

Transmission
Hydraulically-operated diaphragm clutch with 8.5in diameter; four-speed all-synchromesh manual gearbox with optional overdrive (Laycock D-type).

Gearbox ratios

Top	1.00:1
Third	1.25:1
Second	1.78:1
First	2.65:1
Reverse	3.10:1
Overdrive	0.802:1
Final drive ratio	3.27:1 (non-overdrive) or 3.89:1 (overdrive)

Suspension and steering

Front	independent, with twin wishbones, coil springs, anti-roll bar and telescopic dampers
Rear	1970–72: independent 'Rotoflex' type, with reverse lower wishbones, radius arms, transverse leaf spring and telescopic dampers
	1973–74: independent, with transverse leaf 'swing spring,' swing-axles, radius arms and telescopic dampers (from KE 20001)
Steering	rack and pinion, with 4.3:1 ratio
Tyres	155 SR 13 radial

Triumph GT6 Mk3 (1970–73) *(continued)*	
Wheels	four-stud steel type standard centre-lock wire type optional
Rim width	4.5in
Brakes	
Type	discs at the front drums at the rear
Size	disc diameter 9.7in drum diameter 8in, width 1.25in (width 1.5in from KC 20000)

Dimensions [in(mm)]

Wheelbase	83(2,108)
Track, front	49(1,245)
Track, rear	1970–72: 49(1,245) 1973–74: 50(1,270)
Overall length	149(3,785)
Overall width	58.5(1,485)
Overall height	47(1,195)
Unladen weight	2,030 lb/921kg

WHAT THE BRITISH PRESS SAID ABOUT THE GT6 MK 3

The major British motoring magazines did not rush to get their hands on a GT6 Mk 3 to test. The car was, after all, primarily a facelifted version of one they had already tested and liked. This lack of interest may have been the reason why Triumph fielded just one demonstrator, registered as TWK 175 J; although it was strange that this car should have been a four-speed example with the high 3.27:1 overall gearing rather than the lower-geared and more popular overdrive model.

It was *Motor Sport* which was the first to publish its road impressions of the car in February 1971. It thought that it was 'undoubtedly one of British Leyland's better cars', and liked the new styling. Although too heavy to give sensational performance, the GT6 was 'a very brisk car which leaves the line very smartly and puts the power down well.' Good mid-range

acceleration was available, but the brakes lacked feel and needed high pedal pressures. There were detailed criticisms too: the steering wheel was too big, the fuel gauge was masked by the driver's hand and the ignition switch was poorly located.

Autocar echoed many of these points when it came to test TWK 175 J for its issue dated 23 September 1971. The testers thought that the car looked much better than the Mk 2 model. They found the steering light and quick, and the handling was predictable even in the wet. The ride was rather turbulent, but better than the Spitfire's. On the negative side was the poor braking feel, although the car performed well in measured braking tests. The standard Britax Twin-Lok static safety belts were difficult to adjust and uncomfortable to wear, and the starter switch 'seems to have been situated with a view to convenience of installation rather than of use'.

The last major magazine to try out the

GT6 Mk 3 was *Motor*, which published the results of a brief test in its issue of 6 November 1971. The brakes once again proved unimpressive, and this time tended to lock one wheel at a time. Handling was considered to be adequate but not very sporty, and the cornering power proved to be little better than that of many saloons. The ride, too, was rather crashy on secondary roads, while the gearbox whined and the gearchange was occasionally baulky. The safety belts came in for criticism, both because they were hard to adjust and because, when fastened, they prevented the driver from reaching some of the controls. The *Motor* testers thought that it would be worth paying extra to have the optional overdrive, but on the whole they were satisfied with the car. 'Its strong points', they concluded, 'are performance allied to economy and excellent accessibility for d-i-y service.'

Sadly, the 1973-model GT6 with its numerous revisions was never tested by one of the major British magazines. Once again, the problem was that the GT6 was by now an old model and news of minor improvements – however worthwhile – was not going to sell more copies of any motoring magazine.

THE GT6 MK 3 IN THE USA

The 'GT6+' name had suited the American market well, but with the introduction of the Mk 3 models the importers returned to using the standard nomenclature. So the Federal GT6 Mk 3 was called exactly that.

It was also recognizably the same car as the GT6 Mk 3 built for the rest of the world. From the beginning, however, the Federal models had the same high-back seats with fixed head restraints as the Mk 2 cars. They also had side marker lights, thin-band, whitewall tyres, and – inevitably – detuned engines. While the 1971 models were not too badly off, with 90bhp at 4,700rpm and 116lb.ft at 3,400rpm, power and performance nose-dived for the 1972 season. The 1972 and the 1973 cars were so stifled by the detuning and other emission-control measures that they could muster just 79bhp at 4,900rpm and 97lb.ft at 2,900rpm. Triumph appears not to have released any official performance figures, but there can be no doubt that the final Federal GT6s were no longer capable even of 100mph (160km/h).

WHAT THE AMERICAN PRESS SAID ABOUT THE GT6 MK 3

The American press in general saw no need to retest the GT6 during the 1970s. The car had made its mark in the late 1960s and, from the American point of view, it was now past its best because performance was going down as emissions regulations stifled engine power. Nevertheless, *Motor Trend* magazine did sample a GT6 Mk 3 alongside a 1,296cc Spitfire Mk IV and a TR6 and published its findings in March 1972.

This was, of course, a 90bhp car and not one of the later 79bhp examples. It was also a non-overdrive example with the taller 3.27:1 gearing. The emission-control equipment made the engine feel 'mushy' under 3,000rpm, but it still mustered 'healthy mid-range torque'. The estimated top speed was 110mph (177km/h), and 60mph came up in just over 12 sec from a standing start. As the report noted, the lower-geared overdrive car would probably knock up to one second off that time. This was not a bad performance at all.

Despite its origins in the humble Spitfire and its relatively low price, *Motor Trend* considered the GT6 Mk 3 to be 'a true GT ...

This is a Federal or American model GT6 Mk 3, showing the side marker lamps used on cars for that market. It is interesting that this car has the black wheel centres associated with the Spitfire rather than the chromed ones normally seen on the GT6.

it will go like, feel like and do like a number of other cars costing considerably and significantly more.' What a shame, then, that the 1972 and later cars were no longer able to live up to those claims ...

RIVALS

The MGB GT continued to be the GT6's main rival during this period, and no manufacturer introduced a new model to compete in this sector of the market.

Performance figures: GT6 Mk 3

An overdrive-equipped GT6 Mk 3 was capable of around 110mph (177km/h) and 0–60mph in about 10 sec. The higher-geared, non-overdrive cars had a slightly higher top speed but were a little slower through the gears. Fuel consumption was around 30mpg (9.4l/100km) with either transmission, although the overdrive cars had the potential to be less thirsty on long journeys.

The Federal GT6 Mk 3 was slower, taking around 12.5 sec to reach 60mph from rest and reaching a maximum speed of about 104mph (166km/h). Fuel consumption was also poorer than that of the non-Federal cars.

---

8   Spitfire 1500 (1974–80)

Most Triumph enthusiasts outside the USA tend to ignore the fact that the 1,493cc engine was introduced in the Spitfire over there a full two years before it became available in Spitfires for the rest of the world. However, for the sake of tidiness it is certainly easier to view the 1973–74 Federal 1500s as variants of the Mk IV, and to consider the life of the 'proper' 1500 as beginning in December 1974, when the bigger engine was fitted to all new Spitfires.

The circumstances of the 1500's launch make clear that everything was geared to the car's introduction to the USA, however, and they also once again make it difficult to understand the strategy behind British Leyland's publicity in the first half of the 1970s. The 'new' 1500 was to be launched in the USA as a 1975 model at the very end of 1974, and so production was geared to that date. To keep everything orderly, the car was to be announced for the rest of the world during December, with its availa-

bility commencing immediately. So the 1974 Earls Court Show came and went in October with no sign of the new model. This in itself was questionable, as manufacturers regularly use autumn motor shows to preview a car which will not be available before the start of the new year and British Leyland could surely have done the same. However, three weeks later at the Turin Motor Show the British Leyland stand boasted a Spitfire 1500 – without any warning to the media!

To the casual observer, the new Spitfire 1500 looked much like a Spitfire Mk IV, the only obvious visual differences being in the badging. Whereas Mk IVs (and the 1973–74 Federal 1500s) had carried plate badges on the bonnet and rear wings, the 1500s had large decals on the bonnet and the boot lid proclaiming what they were. A closer look would have shown that there were several detailed differences as well. The wheel centres were silver rather than

Top up or top down, the Spitfire 1500 looked very similar to the Spitfire Mk IV it replaced. However, a closer look would reveal silver wheel centres (instead of black) and the absence of rear wing badges.

The identifying badges were now decals on the bonnet and boot lid. Note that the Triumph name was applied only to the rear of the car ...

... where it rather unnecessarily duplicated the badging on the number-plate lamp plinth.

black and the trim round the edges of the rear panel was black rather than chrome. Inside, the dashboard now carried a seat-belt warning lamp and a hazard-warning-lights switch, and the door sills were embellished with polished aluminium tread-plates. The seats had plastic blanking plugs in the top surfaces of their backs, unless the optional head restraints were fitted, and all soft-top cars came with a black tonneau cover as standard.

Other changes were not so visible. There were stiffer front road springs, an automatic boot lamp and an electric rev counter in place of the cable-driven type. Under the bonnet, the new engine was visually very similar to the old; but it had a new exhaust manifold leading to twin downpipes and underneath the chassis frame had been cut away slightly to make room for these. In addition, the right-hand engine valance now had a straight top rather than the indented one of the Mk IV models.

The Spitfire 1500 was also offered with a new Luxury Pack at extra cost. British Leyland marketing at this stage had recognized the value of selling groups of accessories at a cost lower than that of their contents when bought individually, and the Luxury Pack was its application to the Spitfire. It consisted of inertia-reel seat belts (the standard type were static), head restraints, a universally-jointed map light on the passenger's side, a driver's door mirror and a central arm-rest which sat on the transmission tunnel and was accompanied by a saddle of additional trimmed padding.

As for the engine, it was, of course, in a different state of tune from the version seen in the 1973–74 Federal models.

A new steering wheel and houndstooth-check upholstery were introduced together in March 1977. The new wheel had metal spokes; this is actually the similar design with plastic-covered spokes introduced in January 1979. Headrests were standard on all Spitfire 1500s.

Between the square-spoked wheel with exposed metal spokes and the type with plastic-covered spokes, the Spitfitre 1500 came with this Moto-Lita wheel, seen here on a left-hand drive car. It was first used in mid-1978 and has a leather-covered rim. At its centre is the BL wheel logo.

Instead of their single Stromberg caburettor and 7.5:1 compression ratio, it had twin 1.5in SUs with a 9.0:1 compression. This resulted in 71bhp at 5,500rpm and 82lb.ft of torque at 3,000rpm instead of 57bhp at 5,000rpm and 73lb.ft of torque at 3,000rpm. It also represented a useful power increase over the last 1,296cc Mk 3 models too, which were rated at 61bhp at 5,500rpm and 68lb.ft at 2,900rpm. The 1,493cc engine's better torque allowed the final drive ratio to be raised to 3.63:1, gearing which was shared with Triumph's Dolomite 1850 saloon and with the Morris Marina. The gearbox's internal ratios remained unchanged, although the gearbox itself was a new one which had been designed for use in models right across the

British Leyland range. Derived from the old Triumph Toledo gearbox, which had been used in the Mk 3 Spitfire, it was nevertheless slightly longer and incorporated a single-rail selector mechanism in place of the more complicated three-rail type of the earlier gearbox. The optional overdrive was once again Laycock's J-type, and the combination of new engine and taller gearing made the production Spitfire into a genuine 100mph car for the first time.

WHAT THE BRITISH PRESS SAID

'Were it not for the lucrative American market, British-built volume production

The 1,493cc engine looked similar to the older 1,296cc type. Note the straight top to the left-hand valance panel, below the air cleaner.

The last Spitfire of all

The last Spitfire to be made was a British-market overdrive model, finished in Inca Yellow and fitted with a hardtop. Its Commission Number was TFADW5AT-009898. The car was registered as ORW 756 W and is now in the Heritage Collection at Gaydon.

The very last Spitfire of all was built in August 1980 and is now in the Heritage Collection.

sports cars just would not exist', reported *Motor*, in its issue of 24 May 1975. The occasion was a comparison test between the Spitfire 1500 and the MG Midget, which now had the same engine and gearbox as a result of the rationalization within British Leyland. So at least the more knowledgeable members of the British motoring press knew the score on the Spitfire!

On this occasion the Spitfire came out on top, although *Motor* had many kind words to say about the Midget as well. Broadly speaking, though, the Midget was an old-school type of car, while the Spitfire was better-equipped and altogether more sophisticated. In an earlier brief appraisal of the Spitfire 1500 on 7 December 1974 *Motor* had expressed considerable enthusiasm for the car. The staff writer Philip Turner found the new gearbox a pleasure to use, and wrote that the extra torque of the bigger engine 'has vastly improved the traffic performance of the car by making it much more flexible in third and top as well as giving it greatly improved acceleration.' He found the ride 'surprisingly comfortable over uneven road surfaces', and noted that the front spoiler was effective in holding the car on line at speed.

On 1 March 1975 *Autocar* published its findings on a Spitfire 1500, and once again the test staff were enthusiastic about the car. 'In this revitalised form', it summarized, 'the Spitfire 1500 has a lot to offer which no other car quite matches.' And, it added, 'the remarkable fact is that this ever-popular little sports car still seems thoroughly up to date, although its original design is now 12½ years old.'

The testers found that acceleration times had been cut by a big margin and that the Spitfire was now truly capable of 100mph (160km/h) – although this speed was achieved on direct top gear and could not be maintained in overdrive top. The high gearing ensured that there was no mechanical stress during high-speed cruising, but it also meant that the gearbox had to be used quite often at lower speeds. It would have been helpful, the testers thought, to have overdrive operating on second gear as well, in order to cover the large gap between gears. They also considered that overdrive was an essential option.

The new engine added half a hundredweight (56lb, 25.5kg) of weight over the front wheels, but this led to nothing more than a mild increase in understeer. The car had responsive handling and its steering accuracy was 'delightful'. However, it suf-

fered from more scuttle shake than the Mk IV tested some time earlier and its ride was 'decidedly choppy and lively on poor road surfaces'.

After this, the motoring press rather lost interest in the Spitfire. There were no important changes to write about and road tests of an elderly and unchanged model were not newsworthy. So those who planned to buy a Spitfire 1500 in the second half of the 1970s had to rely on these original tests for expert opinions.

PRODUCTION CHANGES TO THE SPITFIRE 1500

The Spitfire 1500 lasted in production for six years, during which period more than 90,000 of them were built. Those statistics make it the longest-lived and the most numerous of all the Spitfire variants, although this was more a reflection of British Leyland's difficulties than of the excellence of the final Spitfire variant. The fact is that the Spitfire really should have been developed more than it was during the 1970s, and the main reason it was not developed more was the cost of keeping it saleable in the USA.

There was no doubt that the Spitfire depended for its existence on sales across the Atlantic. Some 80 per cent of all cars built were being sold in the USA, and it was therefore vital to ensure that sales there held up. However, American emissions and safety legislation became tighter and tighter as the years went on and Triumph (in common with every other car maker selling products in the USA) was obliged to keep on modifying the car so that it complied with the latest legislation. This was extremely costly and it absorbed all the budget which the cash-strapped British Leyland could make available for the car.

Paint and trim colours: Spitfire 1500

All cars had the code numbers of their original body and trim colours stamped on to their Commission Number plates. Where known, these code numbers are given in brackets in the lists which follow. In some cases the same code number was used for both the body colour and the trim colour. In the late 1970s some code numbers changed; in such cases both the early and the late code are shown.

October 1974 – February 1977
Triumph again fielded a range of ten paint colours, of which only five were carried over from the Spitfire Mk IV. The new ones were British Racing Green, Delft Blue, Java Green, Maple Brown and Topaz Orange. There were now just two trim colours.

Body colour	*Upholstery colour*
British Racing Green (75)	beige or black
Carmine Red (82)	beige or black
Delft Blue (136)	beige or black
French Blue (126)	black
Java Green (85)	beige or black
Maple Brown (83)	beige or black
Mimosa Yellow (64)	beige or black
Pimento Red (72)	black
Topaz Orange (84)	beige or black
White (19)	beige or black

March 1977 – August 1980
The final Spitfires were available in a reduced range of seven colours, of which only Carmine Red was carried over from the previous range. The same two trim colours as before were offered, although seat trim was now in houndstooth check. The combinations were:

Body Colour	*Upholstery Colour*
Brooklands Green (HAE)	beige
Carmine Red (82/CAA)	beige
Inca Yellow (94/FAB)	black
Leyland White (NAF)	beige or black
Pageant Blue (JAE)	beige or black
Russet Brown (93/AAE)	beige
Vermilion Red (CAE)	black

The result was that there was no money left to develop a sixth-generation Spitfire.

Over the six years of 1500 production there were, nevertheless, many modifications made to the car, of which the most notable were a group of changes effected in March 1977. Some of these reflected changes made to suit the American market or to meet new regulations in other countries, while others resulted from component rationalization with other British Leyland models. Existing options were also made standard as time went by.

The earliest Spitfire 1500s had BL badges on both front wings, but from October 1975 it appears to have been policy

---

Performance figures: Spitfire 1500

A Spitfire 1500 without the burden of emissions controls could just about reach 100mph (160km/h) in overdrive top gear, and slightly less if overdrive were not fitted. To reach 60mph from rest took just over 13 sec and the overall fuel consumption was likely to be around 35mpg (8.1l/100km).

The Federal Spitfire 1500s were, of course, rather slower. Figures for the later cars are not available, but the 71bhp single-Stromberg cars had a top speed in the mid-90s (about 150km/h) and would accelerate to 60mph in about 15.5 sec – roughly as fast as a Spitfire Mk 2. Fuel consumption was about 30 miles per US gallon. The later cars with less powerful engines were both slower and thirstier.

---

to fit one only to the driver's side wing. Then, during 1976, cars started appearing without them at all, probably because Triumph recognized that owners did not want to be associated with the bad publicity which then surrounded British Leyland.

A driver's door mirror and laminated windscreen became standard equipment quite early on, and then the Luxury Pack was standardized in January 1976. Wiper arms, door mirrors and door-handle escutcheons changed to black (though not all at the same time), and loop-pile carpet replaced the earlier, tufted type. The original carburettors were changed to a tamper-proof type (to meet European emissions regulations), and then a third and yet a fourth type were fitted, the last also having a new air-filter box.

The March 1977 changes brought TR7-style switchgear to replace the original Herald-derived items, and the keylock for the ignition and the steering-column lock was relocated more accessibly. At the same time there was a new electric windscreen washer and the upholstery material changed to feature a combination of houndstooth check (in beige or black) with vinyl. The steering wheel was also changed for one without slots in its flat spokes, but this lasted only until mid-1978 when a Moto-Lita type was fitted. This in turn later gave

way to a more chunkily-styled type.

Other changes included the addition of a courtesy light on the passenger's side, larger diameter brake cylinders on the rear wheels, a viscous coupling for the engine cooling fan and the replacement of the plinth on the rear bumper by twin number-plate lamps mounted in the bumper itself. A clearer speedometer was also introduced, with the speeds marked in numbers every 20mph and the intervening increments marked only by a line. The 1979 model-year cars had wider wheels with 5in rims, and the American-style, dual-circuit braking system was standardized in January 1979. The very last cars had a passenger's side door mirror as standard, together with rear fog-guard lamps mounted under the bumper in order to meet new lighting regulations.

THE SPITFIRE 1500 IN THE USA

The Spitfire 1500s made for the American market once again had a single Zenith-Stromberg carburettor instead of the twin SUs which featured on the cars for all other markets. Coupled to a 7.5:1 compression ratio, this kept their power outputs down to 57.5bhp at 5,000rpm, while torque peaked

---

Triumph Spitfire 1500 (1974–80)

Layout
All-steel bodyshell bolted to steel backbone-frame chassis; two-seater open sports car, with front engine and rear-wheel drive.

Engine

Block material	cast iron
Head material	cast iron
Cylinders	four, in line
Cooling	water
Bore and stroke	73.7mm × 87.5mm (2.90in × 3.44in)
Capacity	1,493cc (91.1 cu.in)
Valves	overhead, two per cylinder
Compression ratio	9.0:1
	1974–76 US models: 7.5:1
	1977–79 US models: 9.0:1
	1980 US models: 7.5:1
Carburettors	two SU type HS2E (1.25in)
	single Zenith-Stromberg IV on US models
Max. power	71bhp at 5,500rpm
	57.5bhp at 5,000rpm, 1974–79 US models
	53bhp at 5,000rpm, 1980 US models
Max. torque	82lb.ft at 3,000rpm
	75lb.ft at 2,000rpm, 1974–79 US models
	69lb.ft at 2,500rpm, 1980 US models

Catalytic converter in exhaust system on US models, 1977 on

Transmission
Hydraulically-operated diaphragm clutch with 6.5in diameter; four-speed all-synchromesh manual gearbox with optional Laycock J-type overdrive.

Gearbox ratios

Top	1.00:1
Third	1.39:1
Second	2.16:1
First	3.50:1
Reverse	3.99:1
Overdrive	0.797:1
Final drive ratio	3.63:1

Suspension and steering

Front	independent, with twin wishbones, coil springs, anti-roll bar and telescopic dampers
Rear	independent, with swing-axles, radius arms, transverse leaf spring and telescopic dampers
Steering	rack and pinion, with 3.75:1 ratio
Tyres	155 SR 13 radial

Wheels	four-stud, steel type standard
	centre-lock wire type optional
Rim width	4.5in (5in on 1979 and 1980-model cars)

Brakes

Type	discs at the front
	drums at the rear
Size	disc diameter 9in
	drum diameter 7in, width 1.25in

Dimensions [in(mm)]

Wheelbase	83(2,108)
Track, front	49(1,245)
Track, rear	50(1,270)
Overall length	149(3,785)
	1979–80 US models: 157.5(4,000)
Overall width	58.5(1,486)
Overall height	47.5(1,206)
Unladen weight	1,750 lb(794kg)
	1,828 lb(829kg) 1975–77 models for USA
	1,850 lb(839kg) 1978–79 models for USA
	1,875 lb(850kg) 1980 models for USA

at 2,000rpm with 75lb.ft. When California demanded catalytic converters in the exhaust systems of all new cars for 1977, Triumph decided against producing a Californian and another version of the same car for all the other American states, and instead fitted all American Spitfires with a catalytic converter. With the engine compression ratio now raised to 9.0:1, the same power and torque outputs as before were claimed.

However, new regulations for 1980 saw the compression ratio reduced to 7.5:1 once again, and power dropped to 53bhp at 5,000rpm while torque went down to 69lb.ft at 2,500rpm. In that year California tightened its emissions regulations even further; Triumph could not make the Spitfire's engine comply and so the car was withdrawn from Californian showrooms.

In most other respects, the American cars were not very different from their counterparts for the rest of the world, since specifications had been growing closer to simplify production. However, the cars did have dual-circuit braking systems from the start, with a front-to-rear split, and they also carried marker lights on the sides of the front and rear wings. For 1980 they were also afflicted with huge over-riders designed to withstand a 5mph (8km/h) impact, which did nothing for the appearance of the Spitfire despite the best efforts of Triumph's stylists. The 1980 cars also had bright wheel-rim embellisher rings (which were also fitted to a small number of other British models), and it seems likely that a small number of the final cars may have carried the 85mph (136km/h) speedometer which became mandatory in the USA under regulations which came into force over the summer of 1980.

The earliest of the American-specification 1500s still had chromed bumpers, even though they were half-hidden by those massive over-riders ...

WHAT THE AMERICAN PRESS SAID

Back in May 1973, when *Road Test* had reported on an early Spitfire 1500 (one of the Federal models contemporary with the Spitfire Mk IV for other markets), the magazine had concluded that 'of the cars in its class the Spitfire is probably the best'. Just three years later, when *Road and Track* included a 1977-model Spitfire in a six-car comparison test for its June 1976 issue, there was no doubt that more modern designs were making the Spitfire look old. But the testers still liked the car more than the MG Midget and MGB they evaluated at the same time. 'Although it has its failings', they concluded, 'these days the Spitfire is the cheapest way to get into an acceptable new sports car.'

The report enumerated some of those failings, too. As the only car in the comparison test with a separate chassis, it was 'not as solid-feeling as the unit-body cars'. Its engine was 'as rough as old boots when revved above 5,000rpm ... and it's noisy as

... but the final examples had all-plastic bumpers, as on this 1980 model. Note also that the British Leyland symbol is not fitted to the front wing of this car.

well in the upper speed ranges.' However, it did give 'peppy performance otherwise, especially in the lower three gears.'

When the Spitfire was in its final year, a *Road and Track* Special took a last look at it and probably reflected the feelings of many American enthusiasts in the affection it expressed for this by now elderly car. 'Even today', the testers said, 'the Spitfire looks pleasant and fully in tune with the times. In fact one could safely say it looks better than ever, thanks to styling and trim details that have been updated with skill – including the latest US bumpers, which

though very bulky do blend in well with the overall shape.' Even though the 53bhp engine was noisy, it still offered 'performance in keeping with the car's character'. The differential on the test car was noisy too, and there was plenty of shaking and rattling from the structure. Despite the testers' obvious affection for the car, however, they had to admit the truth: the Spitfire now had 'modest performance and not particularly tempting handling qualities'. The Spitfire might have grown old gracefully, but there was no denying its age or that other designs offered more.

RIVALS

These were not good times for the traditional, two-seat, open sports car, which had been dependent for three decades on an American market which now seemed to be turning against it. The problem was not a lack of interest among buyers, but had more to do with the manufacturers' fears that the legislation-happy Americans would outlaw open cars sooner or later in their pursuit of road safety. The new models which appeared in the mid-1970s, such as the Triumph TR7 and the Jaguar XJ-S, were closed coupés, and the major manufacturers shied away from introducing new open models.

So the Spitfire did not have to contend with any new direct competitors during the 1970s; but it did have to contend with a different type of competitor in the shape of the Fiat X1/9, introduced in 1973. This featured an advanced mid-engined layout and safe open-air motoring with its detachable roof panel, and was a very tempting and characterful alternative to the traditional, British open roadster. Otherwise, the only real competition came from the Spitfire's in-house rival, the MG Midget.

THE END OF THE ROAD

Throughout the Spitfire's production history the car had been heavily dependent on sales in the USA. By the end of the 1970s some 80 per cent of cars built every year were being shipped across the Atlantic and, as noted earlier, Triumph had spent all the development money available for the car on ensuring that it met the increasingly stringent American safety and emissions regulations. So it should be no great surprise that American developments were also responsible for the car's premature demise in August 1980.

The original plan had been to keep the Spitfire in production until 1982, and to that end its assembly lines might have been transferred from Canley to part of the huge Rover plant at Solihull – which had never been filled by the SD1 saloon for which it had been built. However, before any of this could be properly organized, Triumph ran up against a problem.

Since the mid-1970s California had gone its own way with traffic regulations, notably tightening up on exhaust emissions and insisting that all new cars should be fitted with catalytic converters long before these were obligatory in the remain-

---

Identification and production: Spitfire 1500

The Commission Number of a Spitfire 1500 is in the same place as on earlier models. The numbering sequences were:

FH 75001 onwards (all markets except the USA)
FM 28001U onwards (American models; Californian models have a UC suffix)
VIN numbers (see separate box) from October 1979

The accepted production total for Spitfire 1500s is 91,137, although this figure cannot be considered definitive because there are some inconsistencies in the Triumph production records.

Spitfire 1500 engines have numbers prefixed by FM and the gearboxes and final drives have an FR prefix.

The nationalization of British Leyland

The results of the amalgamation of Triumph and Rover in 1971, and of the reluctant participation in this union of Jaguar from 1972, were endless confusion about management responsibility and a serious decline in morale among the workforce. None of this was helped during 1974 by a three-day working week imposed when a shortage of coal resulting from a miners' strike affected the whole of British manufacturing industry. Product quality suffered, and British Leyland's apparent inability to come up with new products quickly enough to stave off advances made by foreign manufacturers soon led to a serious decline in sales. The first oil crisis in 1973–74 and the fuel price rises which followed hit the sales of big cars badly, and British Leyland suffered further.

By the end of 1974 the situation had become critical, and British Leyland was obliged to go cap-in-hand to the government to seek financial help in order to avoid complete collapse. Nationalization followed, and the government commissioned its industrial adviser Sir Don Ryder to report on the future of what was now known as British Leyland Ltd. Ryder's report was ready by the summer of 1975 and contained a number of recommendations, but many of these were thrown out in subsequent squabbling over BL's future.

One result of this turmoil was that Triumph was severely short of funds in the 1970s. The marque had already spent large sums on developing the TR7 range, introduced in 1975, and so there were other and more deserving causes to which any spare funds would be allocated in the short term. The Spitfire, which was still selling well, was therefore a long way down the priorities list for development money. The result was that the only real development done on the Spitfire after 1974 was that necessary to meet American emissions regulations.

VIN numbers

In October 1979 British Leyland started using standardized VIN (Vehicle Identification Number) codes. These consisted of eight-digit identifying prefixes followed by six-figure serial numbers. The VIN was carried on the car's Commission Number plate and, on the final cars, stamped into the right-hand boot gutter as well. A typical Spitfire VIN would be TFADW5AT009898 (which was actually the last-of-line car, built in 1980). This breaks down as follows:

T	Triumph (make)
F	Spitfire (model range)
A	British or European market
	(Canadian market code was L; US Federal market code was V; Californian code was Z)
D	Drophead (all cars had this letter, even when supplied with a hardtop)
W	1,493cc engine
5	right-hand-drive with overdrive
	(right-hand drive non-overdrive cars were coded 1; left-hand drive overdrive code was 6, and left-hand drive non-overdrive code was 2)
A	1979 and 1980 models (major specification change code letter)
T	assembled at Canley
009898	serial number

Factory-installed options: Spitfire 1500

Competition brake pads (Ferodo DS 11)
Grease nipple on front upper ball joint
Laminated windscreen (standard from 1978)
Luxury pack (standard from FH 80000)
Overdrive

---

ing states of the Union. For 1980, however, Californian emissions regulations became so tight and so different from those obtaining in the rest of the USA that most manufacturers offered their cars in two different states of tune. As the effect of the tighter regulations was to strangle engine power, California had to put up with a much lower performance than the other states.

When Triumph started preparing the 1980 model-year Spitfires, it quickly discovered that the 1,493cc engine simply could not be made to meet the new Californian emissions standard. There was nothing for it but to withdraw the model from sale in there. Triumph already knew that this was likely to lead to a massive loss of sales, because around half of Spitfire sales in the USA were made on the West Coast. And so it proved: American sales nosedived in the first months of 1980.

Meanwhile, the American dollar was gaining strength against the British pound, with the inevitable effect that British Leyland had to choose between raising showroom prices and cutting profit margins. To raise prices would have hit sales even harder, and the profit margins in the USA were already small, being dependent on large sales volumes. Thus British Leyland decided to withdraw the Spitfire from the USA altogether.

Without the American sales on which it was so heavily dependent, the Spitfire was no longer viable as a product for the rest of the world. It was also by now an old design, and barely competitive with more modern cars from other manufacturers. So the decision was taken to stop production altogether. The last Spitfires were built at Canley in August 1980; the final cars lingered in showrooms until well into 1981.

Dealer accessories: Spitfire 1500

Hard top
Headlamp conversion mask
Hood-stowage cover (for use with hardtop)
Mud flaps (rear wheels only)
Oil cooler
Radio, with speaker and aerial
Skid plate
Soft-top conversion kit (for cars supplied with hardtop)
Touch-in paints
Wooden gear-lever knob

---

9 Spitfire and GT6 in Motor Sport

By the time the Spitfire was introduced in 1962, Triumph was a well-established name in international motor sport. The first 'works' TR2 had appeared in 1954, and throughout the rest of the 1950s the TR models had been at the forefront of the company's competition efforts. They remained so during the 1960s, but almost equal prominence was given to the rallying 2000 (and later, 2.5PI) saloons and to teams of racing and rallying Spitfires in 1964 and 1965.

The GT6, unfortunately, arrived on the scene too late to make an impact as a 'works' racer, although there were plans to create such a car. Nevertheless, GT6s were sponsored by the American importers in road racing, and Triumph put a great deal of effort into Spitfire racing in the USA through into the early 1970s. The achievements of the cars prepared by Kas Kastner and the American enthusiasm shamed the reluctance of the Triumph factory under British Leyland control to try harder with its small sports cars.

In fact, there was a hiccup in the story of the Triumph competitions department. After the Leyland takeover in 1961 it was actually closed down for a time, but in 1962 the engineering chief Harry Webster managed to find enough money for a limited motorsport programme which he believed would be a valuable promotional tool. A new works team was set up in 1962 with Graham Robson as its manager, and during that season and the next entered a number of rallies with TR4s and Vitesses. This early programme was not altogether successful, however, and for 1964 Webster supported proposals put forward by Robson to field a team of 2000s for rough-road rallies, a team of homologated Spitfires for road rallies and a team of lightweight, prototype Spitfires for the Le Mans 24-hour road race.

Work began on designing the new cars in October 1963, even though board approval for the programme was not made until December. In the meantime, to gain some valuable experience of the Spitfire in competitions, the left-hand drive prototype car X692 (412 VC) was entered for a number of events in Britain, with Roy Fidler as its driver. As often as not, engine failure prevented the car from finishing, but it did achieve second overall in the Welsh International Rally and provided the Triumph engineers with a great deal of information about how the Spitfire would behave under the hardest of conditions.

THE LE MANS SPITFIRES

Four Spitfires were prepared by the Triumph engineering department for the competitions department to use in the 1964 Le Mans race. They had experimental chassis numbers X727–X728 and X730–X731 and were registered as ADU 1 B, ADU 2 B, ADU 3 B and ADU 4 B. However, it is not clear which car carried

Triumph gained valuable information about the Spitfire's behaviour in motor sport by entering the long-suffering prototype 412 VC in several events with Roy Fidler at the wheel. By this time the car had been converted to right-hand drive. This picture was taken on the 1964 Welsh International Rally.

which registration number and at least two of the cars (ADU 1 B and ADU 3 B) were replaced by all-new machines after accidents in 1964, even though they retained the same identities. It is not beyond the bounds of possibility that the cars' identities were swapped between races, as happens so often in the world of motor sport!

Weight-saving and good aerodynamics were of vital importance in the search to make these cars as fast as possible. Thus the Le Mans Spitfires had all-aluminium

body shells and were fitted with fastback coupé roofs made of GRP. These roofs were similar to, but not the same as, the type later fabricated in steel for the GT6; the most noticeable difference was that there were no louvres behind the rear side windows. The cars also had special bonnets with the headlamps concealed behind more aerodynamic, transparent covers, their radiator grilles were partly blanked off and the bumpers (but not the over-riders) were deleted. All four Spitfires were finished in

One of the Le Mans cars is seen during the practice sessions at the circuit in April 1964. Triumph had not yet decided to fit headlamp fairings.

British racing green and each had a slightly different white flash across its nose to help the pit crews to distinguish one from another quickly. The weight-saving measures meant that they tipped the scales at between 1,625lb (737kg) and 1,640lb (744kg) at the scrutineering for the 1964 Le Mans event.

As far as the mechanical specification was concerned the Le Mans cars had highly-tuned 1,147cc engines, with prototype, eight-port cylinder heads instead of the Siamese-port type of the production engine.

These heads were made of cast iron for durability and the engines boasted an increased rev range which allowed them to put out 98bhp at 6,750rpm. Allied to the lightweight construction and 3.89:1 axle gearing, this allowed the cars to reach a maximum speed of around 134mph (214km/h). They ran with four-speed, all-synchromesh TR4 gearboxes, had special alloy wheels and a stiffened rear suspension which postponed the onset of the Spitfire's characteristic oversteer. The rear axles were prototype GT6 types, running

The engine of a 1964 Le Mans Spitfire shows off its paired twin-choke Weber carburettors; these engines also had prototype eight-port cylinder heads.

with newly-developed, Salisbury limited-slip differentials.

The Triumph experimental vehicles register records the build date of all four cars as May 1964, although this probably represents the date when they were completed to full Le Mans specification. Two of them – unregistered at the time – appeared at the test day in April 1964, and at this stage both lacked the covered-in headlamps and were still some way from their final engine tune.

For the 1964 event all four cars were taken to the Sarthe circuit, but ADU 4 B was designated as the spare and practice car and did not race. Mike Rothschild had ADU 1 B, where he was partnered by the Triumph-USA star driver Rob Tullius. David Hobbs and Rob Slotemaker had ADU 2 B, and ADU 3 B was crewed by Jean-Louis Marnat and Jean-François Piot.

The Spitfires made a promising showing in this first race and to the great delight of the competitions department they proved thoroughly reliable, even though only one

Le Mans, 1964: the Hobbs / Slotemaker car (ADU 2B) finished twenty-first overall and third in its class.

Le Mans, 1964: the three works Spitfires line up for the traditional start.

car actually finished. The Hobbs/Slotemaker car finished in a creditable twenty-first position with an average speed of 94.7mph (151.5km/h) over the 24 hours – a figure which falls into better perspective when compared with the 92mph (147km/h) *maximum* speed of the contemporary production models. More important as far as results were concerned was that this car also came third in its class, behind a pair of Alpine-Renaults and no fewer than fifteen laps ahead of the nearest rival Austin-Healey Sprite, driven by Baker and Bradley. The other two cars were not so lucky, though. The Rothschild/Tullius car crashed heavily under the Dunlop Bridge only a couple of hours into the race and the Rodrigues/Hudson Ferrari just behind it narrowly scraped past, while Marnat crashed about halfway through the race after a rear-end shunt damaged the tail of his car and allowed exhaust gases to leak into the cockpit. As the July 1964 issue of *Motor Sport* put it,

Overcome by the fumes, he zig-zagged drunkenly all the way from Arnage to the pits area, without hitting anything, or being hit, and then richochetted from bank to bank across the track, and finally crashed at the end of the pits, by sheer good fortune not hitting any passing cars or people in the pit area.

The next appearance of the racing Spitfires was at the Sebring 12-hour race in March 1965, when all four cars were shipped across to Florida for this important American event. This time it was ADU 3 B which sat on the sidelines, while its three sister-cars competed for honours. For this event the cars were fitted with GT6-type gearboxes and were entered as homologated GT models, which meant that they were allowed to have modified brakes and gearboxes and different skin panel materials. Perhaps the American scrutineers were just not familiar with the standard Triumph product, because the team should

Not so lucky at Sebring ... ADU1B is seen after its rollover accident in March 1965.

certainly not have been allowed to get away with its all-aluminium shells.

One way or another, the three Spitfires, still finished in British racing green with white nose flashes, were allowed to run at Sebring, and once again they produced a creditable result which made good publicity for Triumph in the USA. Peter Bolton crashed out of the race in ADU 1 B, but the other two cars went on to take the second and the third place in their class. Much to Triumph's annoyance, the class winner was an MG Midget!

The 1965 Le Mans 24-hour race was the scene of the racing Spitfires' most satisfying result. Four cars were entered and, although two were eliminated, the remaining two took the first and the second place in their class and thirteenth and fourteenth places overall. The cars all had new, lightweight chassis frames made of thinner-gauge metal which saved around 31lb (14kg) in weight; they all had smaller GT6-type gearboxes and smaller rear brakes and they used the aluminium cylinder heads which had been confined to the rally cars during the previous season. Altogether these weight-saving measures led to an

Dubois and Piot took ADU 3B to fourteenth overall and second in class in the 1965 Le Mans event.

average reduction of some 110lb (50kg). The engines had been further developed, too, and now boasted 109bhp as against the 98bhp of the 1964 team. Aluminium heat-shields were fitted to allow the carburettors' trumpet intakes to draw in cool air from the wheelarches rather than hot air from under the bonnet, and there was also a new air duct to keep the occupants cool when the cars were travelling at speeds of up to 140mph (225km/h).

Rob Slotemaker's car, the newly-rebuilt ADU 1 B, crashed at White House corner, and Bill Bradley and Peter Bolton were forced to retire in ADU 2 B after an oil cooler failure caused them to run the engine dry. The best result came from Jean-Jacques Thuner and Simo Lampinen in ADU 4B, who came thirteenth overall and took first place in their class with an average speed of 95.1mph (153.074km/h), while Jean-François Piot brought ADU 3 B in right behind them in fourteenth place and second in class with an average speed of 91.28mph (146.903km/h). Of the fifty-one cars which started the race, only fourteen finished, so the Piot car was also the last one to finish.

This was the last time that the Le Mans Spitfires appeared in the hands of the Triumph works team; but it was not the last time that they were raced. Some of them were lent to a private team to compete in the six-hour relay race at Silverstone. ADU 2 B was eventually sold to Bill Bradley, who raced it in numerous European sports car events, and the much-modified car was rediscovered in the south of France more than twenty years later. Parts of the others were probably cannibalized for the GT6R project, and perhaps also for the cars run by privateers in subsequent years which were prepared and maintained by the factory's competitions department.

THE RALLY SPITFIRES

At the same time as the Le Mans Spitfires were being built up by the engineering department, the Triumph competitions department was preparing five more cars as rally machines. These did not have experimental commission numbers, but the first four were registered in the same

---

British epilogue: Bill Bradley's Spitfires

During 1965 the competitions department also prepared a racing Spitfire for Bill Bradley to use as a privateer in sports car races in Britain and Europe. The car, registered as ERW 512 C, was lent to Bradley by Triumph, but the company provided no official sponsorship for Bradley's racing programme.

In 1966 ERW 512 C was replaced by the former works racer ADU 2 B, which Bradley had driven himself at Le Mans in 1965. Once again, Triumph prepared the car and Bradley paid for its running expenses. ADU 2 B was fitted with the strut-type rear suspension originally prepared for the GT6R (and, indeed, may have used parts from the prototype car). After an accident at the Nurburgring, ADU 2 B was written off and had to be completely rebuilt; many parts came from the Triumph racing programme and it seems likely that one or more of the other works cars would have been cannibalized for spares.

During the 1966 season Bradley won fourteen out of the eighteen races he entered in ADU 2 B, and he set up class lap records at no fewer than six circuits: Brands Hatch, Crystal Palace, Goodwood, Mallory Park, Oulton Park and Snetterton.

The Le Mans Spitfires

ADU 1 B

June 1964	Le Mans: Mike Rothschild/Bob Tullius	no.49
	retired after an accident; a new car was subsequently built to take this identity	
March 1965	Sebring: Peter Bolton/Mike Rothschild	no.65
	crashed (rolled) and subsequently rebuilt	
June 1965	Le Mans: Rob Slotemaker/David Hobbs	no.52
	retired after an accident	

ADU 2 B

June 1964	Le Mans: Rob Slotemaker/David Hobbs	no.50
	finished 21st overall and 3rd in class	
March 1965	Sebring: Bob Tullius/Charlie Gates	no.66
	placed in class	
June 1965	Le Mans: Bill Bradley/Peter Bolton	no.53
	retired with split oil cooler	

ADU 3 B

June 1964	Le Mans: Jean-Louis Marnat/Jean-François Piot	no.65
	crashed; a new car was subsequently built to take this identity	
June 1965	Le Mans: Claude Dubois/Jean-François Piot	no.54
	finished 14th overall and 2nd in class	

ADU 4 B

March 1965	Sebring	no.67
	placed in class	
June 1965	Le Mans: Jean-Jacques Thuner/Simo Lampinen	no.60
	finished 13th overall and 1st in class	

sequence as the Le Mans cars, taking the numbers ADU 5 B to ADU 8 B inclusive. The fifth car was prepared for the Stirling Moss Automobile Racing Team and was registered as ADU 467 B. The four works Spitfires were then joined by a sixth for the 1965 season, this time a left-hand-drive example prepared specially for the Finnish driver Simo Lampinen and registered as AVC 654 B.

For the 1964 season the rally cars were finished in the powder blue which had been the Triumph team colour for the preceding two years. The SMART car, however, was finished in the bright green associated with its own team. All five of the cars used in this season had steel bodyshells (in contrast to the aluminium used on the Le Mans cars) but with lightweight aluminium panels, and they all started out with standard Spitfire hardtops. They ran on wide-rim steel wheels (actually 4.5in types from the Courier van) and used a close-ratio Vitesse gearbox without synchromesh on bottom gear, together with the prototype GT6 rear axles incorporating a limited-slip differential. The engines were also specially tuned, with aluminium, eight-port cylinder heads, a very high compression ratio and small 10mm racing motorcycle

In the beginning, the rally cars ran with ordinary hardtops and just a single driving lamp in the centre of the bonnet. This is Terry Hunter in ADU 7B on the 1964 Alpine Rally.

spark plugs to give the maximum room for bigger valves. This combination made them difficult to start in certain conditions. Maximum power at this stage was 102.5bhp at 7,000rpm.

Their first event was the Alpine Rally in June 1964, when three of the Triumph team cars were entered, together with the SMART car. This initial outing was not a geat success. The Moss car crashed, Jean-Jacques Thuner in ADU 5 B collided with a non-competing car and had to retire and Roy Fidler in ADU 6 B had piston and con-rod troubles on the Rousset and was forced to retire. Terry Hunter and Patrick Lier in ADU 7 B hung on, however, and missed gaining a Coupe des Alpes by one minute before finishing third in their class and

seventh in the GT category.

The next event on the Triumph team's calendar was the *Tour de France* in September, which was a rather different style of long-distance road run punctuated by circuit races. For this the works Spitfires were given fastback coupé roofs similar to those of the Le Mans cars but incorporating a small, hinged, boot lid to meet the regulations for homologated cars – and they would retain these for the rest of their time with the Triumph competitions department. They also took on the Le Mans-style bonnets with covered head-lamps, and were fitted with the big 18gal (82l) fuel tanks also associated with the Le Mans cars. Triumph fitted them – against the rules – with prototype, all-synchromesh gearboxes as well.

Once again, three cars were eliminated before the finish. Val Pirie's SMART car retired with engine failure early on, while Bill Bradley and Roy Fidler in ADU 6 B melted a piston during the warm-up lap for the first race at Rheims. Jean-Jacques Thuner and John Gretener made it much further south, before wrecking the engine of ADU 5 B in the French Alps. The fourth car, however, crewed by Rob Slotemaker and Terry Hunter, went on to take tenth place in the GT category and to win its class. It would almost certainly have done even better if a miscalculation had not caused it to run out of petrol on the tightest of the road sections in the Pyrenees and to be penalized for lateness.

Triumph fielded just two Spitfires for the Geneva Rally a month later, these being ADU 6 B and ADU 7 B, the latter being the successful Slotemaker/Hunter car from the *Tour de France*. Still with their fastback tops, 18gal fuel tanks, and Le Mans-style bonnets, these two cars acquitted them-selves extremely well. Terry Hunter and Patrick Lier brought ADU 7 B home in sec-

Spitfires tackled the Monte Carlo Rally in January 1965. Seen here are Val Pirie's SMART car, ADU 467B, and the works team car, ADU 6B, driven by Rob Slotemaker with Alan Taylor.

ond place overall and won their class, thus contributing to Triumph's win of the team prize (which was shared with a private entrant in a Spitfire). Meanwhile, Thuner and Gretener took ADU 6 B to fifth place overall and second in class.

The RAC Rally was held in November that year, and it followed too closely on the *Tour de France* and the Geneva Rally for Triumph to be able to enter the Spitfires; in any case, the 2000 saloons in the team were considered to be better propositions for this event. Val Pirie nevertheless did enter in the SMART car, but without success. In the meantime, Triumph was sorting out its

team drivers for 1965, and although most of the 1964 team remained on the strength, there was one new signing. This was Simo Lampinen, who had distinguished himself by winning the Finnish 1000 Lakes Rally in a Saab 96. He was used to left-hand-drive cars and wanted to continue driving them, so Triumph prepared a new rallying Spitfire (and a new rallying 2000) specially for his use.

For the 1965 season all the rallying Spitfires ran with fastback tops, and all of them had a new front end with a near-standard radiator grille and auxiliary headlamps in fairings let into the bonnet.

The only left-hand drive works Spitfire was AVC 654B, built for Simo Lampinen. It is seen here in the Alpine Rally during July 1965, when it won the Prototype category.

These had been added because the main (outboard) headlamps were fitted with the latest quartz–halogen bulbs to give a brighter beam, but these new bulbs had only a single filament. The inboard lamps therefore served to provide a long-distance main beam. An additional spot lamp mounted on the nose of the bonnet, plus twin foglamps on the front bumper, ensured that no Spitfire driver was likely to complain of poor visibility at night or in bad conditions.

The first of the 1965 events was the Monte Carlo Rally in January, and Triumph entered three Spitfires: ADU 6 B with Slotemaker and Alan Taylor, ADU 7 B with Hunter and Lier, and AVC 654 B with Lampinen and J. Ahava. The Moss car, ADU 467 B, was also entered but retired before the start. Hunter crashed and Lampinen wrecked his engine, but the Slotemaker/Taylor car went on to finish in fourteenth place overall and second in its class.

Lampinen's was the only works Spitfire to enter the Tulip Rally in May 1965, although it was joined by Val Pirie's ADU 467 B and by a pair of works team 2000s. This was not a successful event for the Spitfires, however. Lampinen retired early with clutch failure, and Pirie did finish, but well down the lists. This was the last event in which her car would run under the agreement between the Stirling Moss team and Triumph.

Ever since the *Tour de France* in September 1964 the rally Spitfires had been running with all-synchromesh gearboxes which, as non-production items, were strictly illegal under the regulations of the classes in which they were entered. There was no great shame in this, because most of the works teams bent the rules in one way or another; but at the scrutineering for the Geneva Rally in June 1965 they were caught out. As a result, the gearboxes had to be changed for standard Spitfire types with unsynchronized first gears overnight, before the event started.

Two cars started in the Geneva Rally and both finished with honours. Thuner and Gretener took ADU 5 B to fifth place overall and a class win, while Lampinen took the left-hand-drive ADU 467 B to second place in its class. However, this would be the last time that the rally Spitfires would appear in this form; Triumph had decided that it would have a better chance if it entered them in the Prototype category, running with a number of non-production items as allowed under the rules.

So for the 1965 Alpine Rally in July, Lampinen's left-hand-drive Spitfire and three of the right-hand-drive cars were equipped with prototype 1,296cc engines; a 1,296cc engine would be announced in the brand-new 1300 saloon a few months later, but it would not become available in Spitfires until the Mk 3 models were introduced some two years later. The new engines gave 117bhp at 7,000rpm – much

more than any production 1,296cc Spitfire ever saw – and they had 97lb.ft of torque at 5,500rpm. This new-found flexibility and power were matched by the 9in rear drum brakes seen on the 1964 Le Mans racers.

The results entirely justified Triumph's decision to go down this route with the Spitfires, because Lampinen in ADU 654 B won the Prototype category and Thuner in ADU 5 B came second to him. The other cars were eliminated, Roy Fidler's car losing a rear wheel after its fixing studs sheared and Slotemaker in ADU 7 B wrecking his engine. At long last, it was beginning to look as if the Spitfires had found their niche in motor sport; but unfortunately this would be the last event for the works rally team.

For 1966 there were to be changes to the Appendix J rules, and these would effectively render the Spitfires uncompetitive. They would have to retain standard cylinder heads, the standard body style and the standard steel body skin, and so the Spitfire rallying programme was abandoned. At the same time the Le Mans racers had been effectively decommissioned, and with this the Spitfires bowed out of works-sponsored competition in Europe.

THE MACAU CAR

Nevertheless, the Spitfire's competitions career was far from over. Its American successes lasted into the early 1970s, and out in Hong Kong a very special, works-prepared racer began its short career towards the end of 1965. This was always known at Triumph as the Macau car.

The car was built by the Triumph competitions department for Walter Sulke, who ran ZF Garages, the Triumph dealership in Hong Kong. It was built by using spare

The Macau car was prepared for an owner in Hong Kong, but eventually wound up in the USA with Kas Kastner; it is seen here when new.

parts and panels for the Le Mans cars and was based on them, but it had a number of special features as well. For a start, it was an open car with a streamlined headrest behind the driver, reminiscent of (and copied from) the Jaguar D-type racers of the 1950s. There was no passenger seat, but instead there was a metal rib running alongside the driver between the scuttle and the rear of the cockpit, and the opening above the passenger seat area was blanked off. The car had a 22.5gal (85l) fuel tank and ran on 5.5in wide alloy wheels. Its

engine was a 109bhp 1,147cc competition unit, and the Macau Spitfire was allegedly capable of more than 130mph (210km/h) even with the low 4.1:1 axle gearing used to give maximum acceleration. On test at the MIRA banked circuit in Britain, it lapped at 122mph (195km/h).

Little is recorded about the car's brief career in Hong Kong, where it appeared in a number of races. By the autumn of 1967, however, its engine would have been unrepresentative of the Spitfire because the new 1,296cc Mk 3 models were on sale,

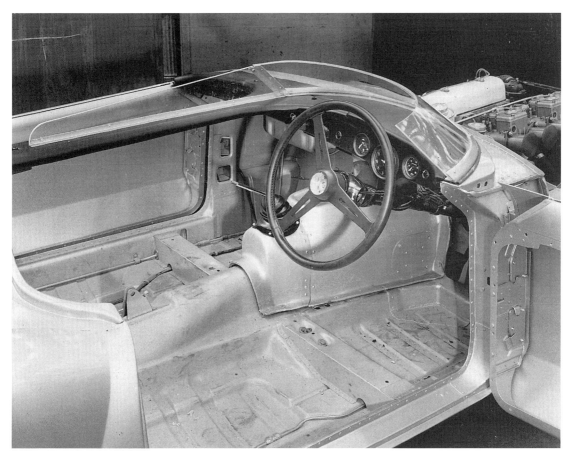

The unique cockpit of the Macau car was pictured here while the car was still under construction. Just visible are the two twin-choke Webers of the 1,147cc race-tuned engine.

and it must have been around this time that it was shipped out to Kas Kastner, mastermind of the Triumph-USA racing effort, in Los Angeles. Kastner immediately fitted a 2-litre GT6 engine with triple Weber carburettors and around 220bhp, added a TR6 gearbox and began running the car in the D-Modified class of events organized by the Sports Car Club of America. Very fast in a straight line, the car nevertheless needed wider tyres to make it competitive. To fit these would have demanded major bodywork modifications, and Kastner had other fish

to fry. Thus the Macau car faded from the scene.

THE GT6R

Triumph's results at the 1965 Le Mans race had been encouraging, but the competitions department knew that there was only a limited amount of development left in the Spitfires. For the 1966 Le Mans race, they would need something radically different if they were to remain competitive. Harry Webster therefore asked the department to

The GT6R was an exciting project, but it was never completed. The six-cylinder engine with its triple twin-choke Weber carburettors is seen here in the car in December 1965.

begin the development of a new racing machine. The intention was to run this in the Prototype category as a 2-litre model, and in effect the car would have foreshadowed the GT6 with its six-cylinder engine and fastback bodyshell which was due to go on sale in the autumn of 1966, some three or four months after Le Mans. There was no doubt that a good result there would give a welcome boost to sales of the new car.

It was known at Triumph as the GT6R, the first part of the name having an obvious derivation and the R presumably standing for 'Racing'. Its body was essentially that of a Le Mans Spitfire, with aluminium panels, streamlined bonnet with faired-in headlamps and, of course, the fastback coupé roof. Under the bonnet was a Triumph 2000 six-cylinder engine, fitted with the new type of cylinder head which would appear on the TR5 and on the GT6 itself, and there were three Weber carburettors. Ray Henderson's competitions department expected 175bhp from this installation, and they hoped at a later stage to replace it with Lucas fuel injection,

The works rally Spitfires

ADU 5 B

June 1964	Alpine Rally: Jean-Jacques Thuner/John Gretener retired after collision
Sept 1964	Tour de France: Jean-Jacques Thuner/John Gretener retired with engine failure
Oct 1964	Paris 1000km race: Jean-François Piot/Jean-Louis Marnat 1st in class
June 1965	Geneva Rally: Jean-Jacques Thuner/John Gretener fifth overall, 2nd in GT category and 1st in class
July 1965	Alpine Rally: Jean-Jacques Thuner/John Gretener 2nd in Prototype category

ADU 6 B

June 1964	Alpine Rally: Roy Fidler/Don Grimshaw retired after engine failure
Sept 1964	Tour de France: Bill Bradley/Roy Fidler retired after engine failure
Oct 1964	Geneva Rally: Jean-Jacques Thuner/John Gretener 5th overall and 2nd in class; team prize (with privately-entered Spitfire)
Jan 1965	Monte Carlo Rally: Rob Slotemaker/Alan Taylor 14th overall and 2nd in class
July 1965	Alpine Rally: Roy Fidler/Graham Robson retired with broken wheel studs

ADU 7 B

June 1964	Alpine Rally: Terry Hunter/Patrick Lier 3rd in class and 7th in the GT category
Sept 1964	Tour de France: Rob Slotemaker/Terry Hunter 10th in GT category and 1st in class
Oct 1964	Geneva Rally: Terry Hunter/Patrick Lier 2nd overall and 1st in class
Jan 1965	Monte Carlo Rally: Terry Hunter/Patrick Lier retired after accident
July 1965	Alpine Rally: Rob Slotemaker/Alan Taylor retired after engine failure

ADU 8 B

This was the spare car in the rally team and was never used in anger.

AVC 654 B

Jan 1965	Monte Carlo Rally: Simo Lampinen/J. Ahava 24th overall and 3rd in class
May 1965	Tulip Rally: Simo Lampinen/J. Ahava retired with clutch failure
June 1965	Geneva Rally: Simo Lampinen/J. Ahava 2nd in class
July 1965	Alpine Rally: Simo Lampinen/J. Ahava 1st in Prototype category

which had already been tried on a Le Mans Spitfire and was part of the forward programme for the road-going TRs as well.

The engine was mated to a 2000/TR4 type of gearbox with overdrive, and the chassis-mounted final drive was also of the 2000/TR4 type. The plan was to fit bigger brakes, wheels and tyres than the Le Mans Spitfires had used, and the competitions staff had made a determined effort to counter the rear suspension's tendency to jack-up and give sudden oversteer. In place of the production swing-axles they had a MacPherson strut independent rear suspension (similar to that in the Lotus Elan), which was mounted within a special

pressed and fabricated cradle that was welded to the chassis frame.

The GT6R project sounded extremely promising, but it was never completed. Work stopped on the single prototype in February 1966 as Triumph wound down its competitions programme and the car was eventually broken up.

SPITFIRE AND GT6 IN COMPETITION IN THE USA

It was during 1962 that Standard-Triumph Inc., the American importers of the Triumph marque, began to recognize the

---

Driving ADU 7 B

'Soon one forgets the strangeness and ... begins to like it in the same way as a cross-country run or a cold shower, for the exhilaration, the challenge and – yes – the wonderful calm and relaxation of being warm by the fireside afterwards.' Thus did Geoffrey Howard sum up his road test of the rally car ADU 7 B in *The Autocar* on 3 December 1965.

The car's competitions career was over by this time, and the prototype 1,296cc engine fitted for its Alpine Rally appearance in July 1965 had been replaced by a Stage 2 Le Mans 1,147cc unit, giving a claimed 105bhp at 7,250rpm and 86lb.ft of torque at 5,500rpm. It still had its prototype, all-synchromesh gearbox, together with the low axle ratio, limited-slip differential, large front calipers, TR4 rear drums, stiff springs with adjustable dampers and wide-rim wheels shod with Dunlop SP3 tyres – all homologated Group 2 rally items. The interior was as it had been on the rallies, with a wrap-around bucket seat for the driver, a more comfortable seat for the co-driver, an oversize brake pedal (taken from a Triumph 2000 Automatic), additional switches on the facia and blacked-out metal surfaces to prevent reflections.

Howard reported that the car was very intractable, with little torque available below 4,000rpm. Together with the high first gear, this made quick getaways impossible, and high indirect gears also made progress difficult unless the engine was revved hard. The professional drivers, he learned, generally kept the engine spinning at between 5,000 and 7,500rpm to get the best out of it. This was not a car which enjoyed being driven in traffic.

Yet the strongest impression it made resulted from its lack of refinement. Howard found it incredibly noisy inside, with the noise from the unsilenced, twin-choke Webers combining with the resonation of the GRP coupé fastback to produce an almost unbearable cacophony. Vibration added to the discomfort.

So it is important to remember that the achievements of the Triumph works rally Spitfires were not only the result of careful preparation by the competitions department. Their drivers, too, needed to be able to deliver their best in conditions which would have worn lesser men down very quickly.

ADU 7 B still survives, now in private hands.

The SMART rally car

This car was prepared by the Triumph competitions department on behalf of the Stirling Moss Automobile Racing Team (SMART) for their driver Valerie Pirie.

ADU 467 B

June 1964	Alpine Rally: V. Pirie/Y. Hilton
	retired after an accident
Sept 1964	Tour de France: V. Pirie/S.Reeves
	retired after engine failure
Nov 1964	RAC Rally: V. Pirie/S. Reeves
	retired
Jan 1965	Monte Carlo Rally: V. Pirie/S. Reeves
	retired – OTL
May 1965	Tulip Rally: V. Pirie/S. Reeves
	finished

The SMART car was later sold to Triumph employee Peter Cox, who won the Freddie Dixon Trophy with it in 1967, and during 1969 – still maintained by Peter Cox and Peter Clarke – it was being raced with some success in club events by Richard Lloyd.

Leading the pack here is Peter Cox, the most successful privateer racing Spitfires in the 1960s.

value of competition successes in selling Triumph sports cars across the Atlantic. In that year the company signed up the former racing driver R.W. 'Kas' Kastner to prepare TR4s for customers who wanted to use them for racing and a team of cars for the importers to race at the annual, high-profile Sebring 12-hour sports car race.

The Spitfire reached the USA in the early spring of 1963, and within a week of the first car's being unloaded on the West Coast an example was entered in a road race where it ran a strong third until forced to retire. Before long many privateers were campaigning Spitfires in Sports Car Club of America (SCCA) events at both the regional and the national level, and the importers made available a range of tuning accessories to meet their needs. By the end of 1963 a Stage 2 engine-tuning kit was on offer, and it was possible to decrease the camber of the rear wheels and to fit a camber compensator (a long cross-bar which ran below the line of the axle) in order to tame the rear end's waywardness under hard cornering. The Spitfires quickly

Among the most successful Spitfire racers in the USA was Brian Fuerstenau.

Mike Downs became SCCA E Production National Champion in 1969 with the Group 44 racing GT6+.

picked up a good reputation for both speed and durability in road racing, and during 1964 the Californian driver Ed Barker brought glory to the marque by winning the GP class of the American Road Race of Champions. Meanwhile, on the other side of the country Bob Tullius was making his mark with a Spitfire in SCCA divisional races.

Things warmed up even more during 1965, when the Le Mans works racers put in an appearance at Sebring, and Triumph were careful to engage the local hero Bob Tullius to drive one of the cars. It was during this year too that the American importers announced a programme of rewarding owners who were successful with Spitfires in divisional and national SCCA events.

Kastner began to work with Spitfires in 1967, when the Mk 3 models became available, and before long turned to GT6 models as well. The original GT6 was never homologated for SCCA racing (although it appears that an open version won the Regional D Sports Racing championship on the West Coast that year). From late in 1967, however, the GT6 was homologated and Kastner got to work on that as well. The first Kastner-tuned GT6 cars put out 185bhp at an incredibly high 8,200rpm. Later versions had the cylinder head from the 2.5-litre engine, and pumped out 218bhp with triple Weber carburettors; but the GT6 did suffer from reliability problems because of a weakness in its rear hubs.

The big name over the next few years in Triumph racing was Bob Tullius's Group 44 team, whose key drivers were Tullius himself, Carl Swanson and Brian Fuerstenau. A Group 44 GT6+ driven by Mike Downs also took first place in the E Production class at Lime Rock in the national SCCA races. However, British Leyland seemed far less interested in competition success in the USA than Triumph had done, and in 1970 Kas Kastner resigned as competitions manager for Triumph's American importers. Nevertheless, he set up a new organization with John Brophy, and Kastner Brophy Racing won the contract to prepare and run the works Triumphs for 1971 and 1972. Among the cars were GT6 Mk 3s and among the drivers was Don Devendorf. However, the operation had closed down by 1973 as the boom period for British sports cars in the USA began to draw to its close.

The Peter Cox Racing GT6

After some success with the ex-Val Pirie Spitfire and further work on Gold Seal-sponsored cars driven by Richard Lloyd and Chris Marshall, Peter Cox decided to turn his hand to racing a GT6. The car he built appeared for the first time in spring 1970 and had been developed for the Group 6 2-litre prototype category. Cox drove the car himself in seven British club events during the 1970 season, achieving one first overall, two class firsts and two class seconds. On both of the car's outings at Thruxton it retired; on the first occasion this was the result of an accident and on the second the result of a blown head gasket.

Only the chassis and the windscreen surround of the Cox car were standard. Wings, doors, bulkhead, floor pan and bonnet (modified with a power bulge) were all aluminium-alloy components from the spares stock for the works competition cars, and the GRP fastback roof was also from the Triumph from works stock. The driving seat too was a Restall type from a works Spitfire. Several other body modifications were carried out by Cox by the use of GRP. The result was an exceptionally light car, weighing just 11cwt (559kg) as against the 17cwt (864kg) or more of the standard production GT6.

The GT6's six-cylinder engine tipped the weight unevenly towards the front, so Cox moved the engine back by 9in (230mm) to get a 50–50 weight distribution for better handling. The engine itself had a flowed and modified cylinder head with larger inlet valves, a special camshaft, three 42 DCOE Weber carburettors and a 12:1 compression ratio. A lightweight alloy flywheel was also fitted. The output was stated to be 183bhp at 7,000rpm.

The rear suspension had modified wishbones and dispensed with the radius arms. It also had a six-leaf spring in place of the standard eight-leaf type, and used Hardy Spicer joints in place of the standard Rotoflex couplings. The final drive had a 3.63:1 ratio with a Salisbury limited-slip differential, and the wheels were Minilites with 8.5in rims, running on Dunlop CR 82 racing tyres.

The car proved very competitive and on one occasion beat the lap record at Silverstone by 2 sec while running-in during practice. However, its wider success was limited by a lack of funds.

The Chris Williams racing GT6

A second racing GT6 appeared on the British club circuit during 1971 and showed considerable promise during that season and the one which followed. The car was prepared and raced in the Modsports category by Chris Williams, a former Standard-Triumph employee who now ran a company called Windmill Plastics.

Windmill Plastics made up an entire bodyshell for the GT6 in GRP, which made the car around 5cwt (254kg) lighter than the standard production type. To improve the weight distribution, the engine was moved back in the frame by nearly 12in (305mm). During 1971 the car was tried out in a few events with the engine in more or less standard tune except for the addition of three 42 DCOE Weber carburettors, and in this guise its biggest failing was found to be its handling.

So over the winter of 1971–72 the rear suspension was replaced by a custom-built, coil-spring design drawn up by the Aldon Performance Centre, and the front suspension was also modified slightly. This proved much better during the early part of the 1972 season. Thus, encouraged by the much improved handling, Williams rebuilt the engine at mid-season with a racing camshaft and a 12:1 compression ratio. By the end of 1972 the powerplant was producing 134bhp, and the car (tested by *Cars and Car Conversions* magazine in January 1973) could reach 60mph from rest in around 6 sec and 100mph (160km/h) from rest in around 15.5 sec on its 4.11:1 final drive.

Chris Williams also made the GRP bodyshell and the coil-spring rear suspension available to other club racers in the early 1970s.

10 Spitfire and GT6 Today

Related they may be – twins almost – but the Triumph Spitfire and GT6 models have quite different characters. A GT6 is most certainly not just a Spitfire with a roof, and a Spitfire is most certainly not just a convertible GT6. The cars' characters are not defined only by their body configurations, because Spitfires are still very different from GT6s even when they are fitted with hardtops. A great deal of the personality of each car is created by its drivetrain. The high gearing and six-cylinder engine of the GT6 make it into a relaxed grand tourer, while the lower gearing and more frenzied four-cylinder engine of the Spitfire make it much more of a nippy little sportabout. This is not the occasion on which to begin an argument about whether the Spitfire is more sporting than the GT6 and whether the GT6 is a sports car at all, but many people do hold strong views on the subject...

Therefore anyone who has read this far and is seriously tempted to buy one of these small Triumphs would do well to think hard about what the car will be used for. If the idea is to have an open sports car, then there is really no question: the choice will have to fall on a Spitfire (although some ambitious and skilled owners have created hybrids by putting GT6 drivetrains into Spitfire bodies). If much high-speed, long-distance motoring is in view, then the GT6 is going to be a better bet. Think too about the importance of overdrive, because not every car of either type has it. Most people view it as an advantage, which explains why overdrive cars tend to be a little more expensive than non-overdrive models.

However, there are those who swear that non-overdrive Spitfires and GT6s are just as practical and just as much fun as overdrive models. In the same vein, how important is a hard top to you if you are buying a Spitfire?

Of course, hardtops can usually be found and added to a car after its purchase, and overdrive may also be added to a non-overdrive car by an owner who knows what he or she is doing, or is prepared to pay for professionals to do the work. However, it is not possible to alter the fundamental character of a car. The Spitfire Mk IV and the 1500 are very different animals from the Mk 1 and the Mk 2 type, and the Mk 3 is an interesting transitional model which is different again. The Mk 3 GT6 is everybody's favourite, but the Mk 1 cars also have a charm of their own, and a Mk 2 (or GT6+ in the USA) combines the later and more powerful engine with the more curvaceous early styling and improved rear suspension. (Most of them also have those dreadful, fake Rostyle wheel trims, but that is perhaps a personal view...)

Buyers in the USA are faced with a rather different set of choices. The difference of badging (GT6+ rather than GT6 Mk 2) is of little importance, but the 1500-engine Mk IV Spitfires complicate the choice by creating yet another model. The fundamental problem, however, is associated with the post-1968 emissions-controlled engines. As the years passed and power and performance dropped alarmingly, so the cars were improved in other ways, with more safety equipment, better interiors and so on. So there is the dilemma. On the one hand, the buyer can go for a later car which will have had less time to deteriorate and will be better equipped but slower. On the other, there are the earlier cars which may not be in such good condition and will have less attractive specifications, but are likely to be faster.

PROBLEMS, PROBLEMS ...

It would probably be fair to say that there is absolutely nothing on one of these cars which cannot be repaired, replaced or refurbished, given the appropriate amounts of time, enthusiasm, energy and money. However, that does not mean that every rusty relic which has lain in a field for the last five years is worth restoring. Neither the Spitfire nor the GT6 is a particularly rare car, and now that they have been espoused by enthusiasts it seems unlikely that either of them ever will be. That in turn keeps the prices of even the best specimens down to quite reasonable levels and has the effect that it is not worth pouring huge amounts of money into a restoration because the job is likely to cost more than it would have taken to buy a good car in the first place. So, the first piece of advice when buying is to be sensible. Really poor specimens of these cars might make good sources of spares, or they might be so bad that they will not even yield useful parts to keep another car on the road. One way or another, though, it is best to start with a car which is fundamentally sound.

It is not too difficult to detect any problems in a Spitfire or a GT6 which is offered for sale. However, some are less easy than others to spot. Sometimes an owner will have devoted much effort to cosmetic restoration, only to find when the money

has run out that there is still a long way to go mechanically – or worse, structurally. That sort of owner will play up the good side of the car and play down the problems which are lurking out of sight. It is thus up to the buyer to look for them, to assess how bad they are and to decide whether they are enough to make the car not worth buying. What the rest of this chapter aims to do is to offer a comprehensive guide to all areas of the Spitfire and the GT6. Armed with this knowledge, any buyer should be able to avoid spending money on the wrong car.

THE BODY

The body is the first thing you see on a Spitfire or a GT6, and every buyer forms a first opinion of the car from its appearance. For that reason sellers tend to concentrate on making the body look as presentable as possible. Sometimes, however, a coat of paint and some polish will be used to deflect attention from faults which range from the irritating to the serious. However, take heart from the fact that the Spitfire's body is less prone to serious corrosion than most contemporary monocoque sports-car bodies. The car's separate-chassis construction also means that major body repair work may be simpler and less expensive than on a monocoque car.

At the front of the car check the front valance panel ends, where stone chipping usually allows rust to get a hold. Replacement panels are available at reasonable cost, so this is not too much of a worry. Some owners have eliminated the problem by fitting non-original panels made from GRP and it is difficult to fault their reasoning on practical grounds. Next, check the bonnet panel very thoroughly. This is a really important part of the inspection because bonnet panels are expensive to replace and – even more important – a misaligned bonnet panel gives an early warning that the car may have been in an accident and that something underneath has not been straightened out properly. Equally, a misaligned bonnet panel which a seller claims to be a new one most probably shows that a little further adjustment is needed. Fitting one of these big panels satisfactorily requires more patience than many people have.

Bonnets rust, and most commonly around the wheelarches and behind the lights. For a proper inspection you should also open the bonnet and examine the inner wings, where rust often gets a hold unnoticed by the average owner. If there is serious bonnet damage a complete replacement panel is probably the best solution. While the bonnet is open, gently try to rock it on its hinges: if there is significant movement the hinge bushes are worn and should be replaced.

With the bonnet still open two other important areas of the body can be checked. The first is the bulkhead, which can rust out at the bottom. Bad rust here will usually also be visible from the footwells inside the car. At the top of the bulkhead the battery tray may also corrode, either because of acid spillage or from simple water penetration of the protective

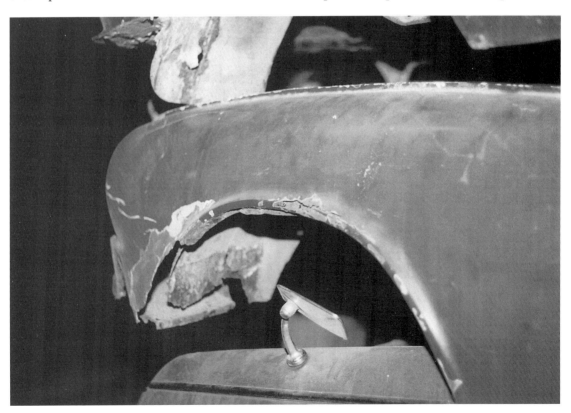

Look for rust around the wheelarches on the large, hinged front panel. This badly affected example was pictured after it had been removed from a car.

Aftermarket GRP replacement bonnets were available for a period, and examples occasionally still turn up. Note, on this example, how the holes for headlights and bonnet catches have to be cut before the panel can be fitted.

This sort of rust damage, on the right-hand side of a Mk 3 Spitfire's front bulkhead, will not be easy to repair.

paint layer. You may need to move the battery to be absolutely certain about the condition of this area. The second area which may give trouble is the bottom of the A-post (windscreen pillar), especially where it attaches to the sill panel. All rust in these two areas can be cut out and repaired, but it takes an expert to make a good clean job of it and that means expense.

It is also worth checking the condition of the windscreen side pillars themselves. On Spitfires particularly, peeling back the door-sealing rubber may reveal quite advanced corrosion which is not visible from the outside. GT6s have their own peculiarity, which is that the lip at the front of the roof panel can rust. Neither the windscreen pillars nor the roof lip is easy to repair neatly. Moving further back, there should be no other problems with the GT6 roof, but the Spitfire's soft top suffers from rotted stitching. The fabric may, of course, tear, and fixing studs can pull out. The plastic rear window becomes yellowed and opaque after a time and, if badly creased

The bulkhead and A-pillar area may suffer badly. Note the tape wrapped around the bonnet catch platform on this Spitfire – not an encouraging sign!

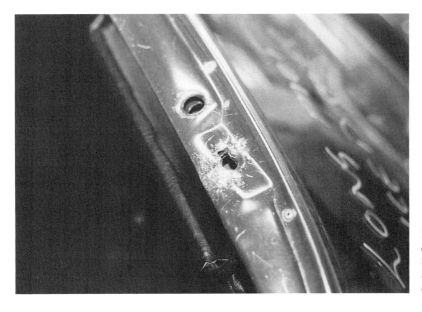

The windscreen top capping may get quite badly damaged by the locating pegs on the soft and the hardtop.

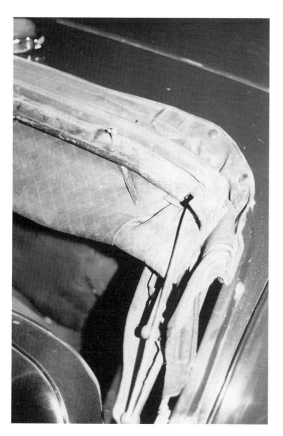

How well has the hood frame worn the passage of time? This one is still clinging on to life, but only just!

Doors should shut properly; this sort of misalignment suggests more serious problems are present.

while stored in the hood well, it may actually split. Lastly, the metal hood frame itself can break, particularly at its pivot joints.

The next area to check is the doors. First of all, they should shut easily and align properly with the wings. If the alignment seems good but the door is hard to close, the problem is likely to be nothing more serious than a misaligned catch. However, if the alignment is poor the problem may well be that the door has dropped on its hinges. Doors rust at the bottom of their outer skins, which can be replaced easily enough. However, there is no point in replacing a rusted outer skin unless the inner shell of

the door is in good condition. Door shells rust at their lower edges, and if there is serious rust here the best solution is to look for a replacement door because repairs may be extremely difficult and costly.

Underneath the doors the sills should also be checked. These are important structural elements and give the body shell most of its strength. At their front ends the closing plates behind the front wheels often rust badly, and it is worth checking the slightly less vulnerable rear ends as well. If a sill does not line up properly with either door or wing the chances are that something serious is amiss. It may be that a

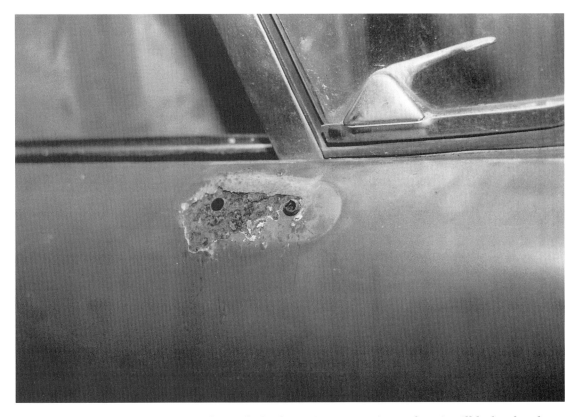

On later cars rust may break out underneath the door mirror mountings, where it will be hard to detect until decay reaches an advanced stage.

replacement sill has been fitted and has been misaligned. Equally, the body may be sagging in the middle because the sill is weak from corrosion. To check for major weakness, open the doors one at a time and lift them gently on their hinges while watching for any movement of the inner sill. Any sign of flexing means that the sill is weak. It is also important to check underneath the car where the sill is attached to the floor pan. Rust may cause the two panels to separate here.

The floor and the footwells deserve a careful examination. Double-check the attachment of the floor to the inner sill by looking at the area from above. The footwells also need a careful examination

because rust gets a hold next to the A-pillar. The area around each safety-belt mounting in the floor must be rust-free for obvious reasons. Perhaps most important here, however, is the heelboard behind the seats. Lift the carpet and check carefully for rust or stress fractures in the panel. The rear suspension trailing arms are bolted to the outside of this panel and it is not unknown for them to tear loose on a badly rusted car, with consequent sudden and dire effects upon the handling.

At the back of the car look for rust all around the wheelarch. There may be rust in front of it as well as in the more usual locations above and behind. The rear wing comes together with both the rear panel and the boot floor at its trailing edge, and this junction is especially vulnerable to rust. Look at the inner wheelarch which may also have started to rust through. This area is most important in the GT6 Mk 2, the GT6+ and the pre-1973 GT6 Mk 3 because the rear damper mountings are attached to the wheelarch panels.

Right at the tail of the car a dented or rippled rear panel suggests that the car has had a rear-end shunt. If similar damage is visible in the boot floor, expect other items to have been poorly repaired as well. The vertical rear panel of the Mk IV and the 1500 Spitfire and the Mk 3 GT6 suffers from corrosion more readily than that on earlier models. Boot lids rust in their rear corners and are very hard to repair satisfactorily; on the later types corrosion often begins under the trim finishers and has got

a firm hold by the time it becomes visible on the main panel. Check the boot-lid hinges on Spitfires too. They can rust and in bad cases may seize and break. In addition, misaligned boot-lid hinges suggest that the panelwork at the rear of the car is not as straight as it should be.

THE INTERIOR

Interiors are generally fairly hard-wearing, and only the most abused cars are likely to have serious defects here. However, many cars have minor defects which spoil an otherwise good appearance. Fortunately, most items, both large and small, can be replaced from the new old stock or remanufactured components carried by the specialists.

Replacement panels of all kinds are available, but they may not always fit as well as the originals. The large gap evident on this early Spitfire 4 reveals that the bootlid is not original.

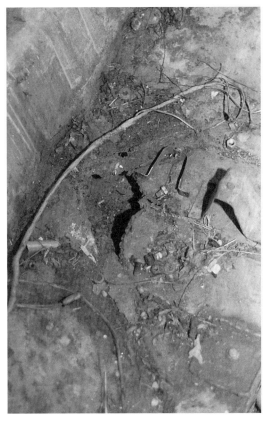

This mess is what used to be the boot floor of a Spitfire 1500. Note how rust has eaten right through the metalwork underneath where the spare wheel normally sits.

All seats begin to sag and lose their shape after a time, but this problem can be dealt with. Much more serious are broken frames and floor fixings which have worked loose; sometimes the holes in the floor pan can elongate, in which case the remedy is a little more complicated than simply to tighten the bolts. The vinyl seat covers can tear and the lighter colours will stain. The contrasting edge piping on some seats may also become detached or damaged so that it exposes the metal core.

The later GT6 seats are upholstered in fabric, which is hard-wearing but does need regular cleaning. Dirt becomes ingrained in the fabric after a time and can be difficult to remove. Leather upholstery is not very common and is therefore well worth resurrecting if it is looking tired. The biggest problem with leather is that it dries out, hardens and begins to crack. Cracks lead to splits and splits lead to tears and, by this stage, the only remedy is replacement, which is expensive. Regular use of hide food will rejuvenate dry leather and make it supple again, although it will not return colour to areas where the underlying brown is showing through. Many people, however, see a certain amount of wear as lending additional charm to a leather interior, so perhaps there is no need to fuss too much about this.

Dashboards are not as hard-wearing as you might think. The vinyl covering on the instrument panel of early cars and the black vinyl which covers the crash padding on later ones can tear. The crash padding on the exposed upper surfaces of the dashboard may also discolour in the sun. While small tears can be neatly repaired using a purpose-made adhesive, discoloration is harder to deal with. There are vinyl paints on the market, but it is difficult to make a good job of recolouring a small area and blending it in with the surrounding material.

Many cars, of course, have a wooden dashboard. This wears well and is not as prone to discoloration and cracking as are its counterparts on many other cars. Light scratches can be blended into the surrounding area by using a furniture scratch-remover polish, but deep scratches may be difficult to cover up. It is extremely annoying to find that an otherwise good dashboard has been ruined by the thoughtless addition of extra instruments for which holes have been cut into the surface. Fortunately, replacement dashboards are available, but their fitting can be quite time-consuming because of the amount of dismantling which has to be done and because of the need to take care when rewiring all the switches, lights and dials. Some cars will, of course, be fitted with instruments or a steering wheel taken from another model of a Spitfire or GT6. In order to be sure of what is correct for any particular car the best thing to do is to check in John Thomason's excellent *Triumph Spitfire and GT6: A Guide to Originality*, published by The Crowood Press. Please note, however, that this book does not cover the unique features of the American models.

Two more points should be checked in the interior of a car. Heaters, where fitted, must work. If the heater does not pump out a reasonable amount of warmth, suspect a faulty water valve which will need attention sooner rather than later. The second point is that some GT6 models were fitted with a fabric sunroof. These may be noisy, and the poorer their fit the noisier they are. They should not leak, and they should slide back and forwards without difficulty: evidence of grease in the channels suggests that the sunroof has been properly maintained. A tinted, plastic, wind deflector was fitted to the front of the sunroof opening on most cars and it should be both present and unbroken. To find replacements is not easy.

It is also important to look inside the boot of a Spitfire and in the luggage area under the tailgate of a GT6. The fibre boarding which forms the floor panels should be in sound condition; as often as not, it has suffered some form of damage. Needless to say, cars with wire wheels should have the appropriate spare in the spare wheel compartment, and there should also be a removal tool for the centre-lock types. For wheels with eared spinners the tool is a soft-faced mallet; for wheels

with hexagonal centre nuts there should be a large, hexagonal spanner.

THE ENGINE

The four-cylinder Spitfire engine and the six-cylinder GT6 type have the same common ancestor, which is the overhead-valve, four-cylinder introduced as early as 1953 in the Standard Eight saloon. All the engines of this family are durable units, without any special faults. However, when road-testing either a Spitfire or a GT6 you should expect to be distinctly underwhelmed by the car's performance. Both were quick enough in their day, but modern cars have come a long way since then. To expect a thirty-year-old, 1,147cc Spitfire to match the acceleration of one of today's 1.2-litre small saloons is quite unreasonable!

For the most part, the problems are likely to be ones of wear, caused by nothing more sinister than a high mileage. Excessive tappet noise is one of the most common faults and suggests that a valve gear rebuild will soon be necessary. Like all overhead-valve engines, timing-chain rattle also suggests a problem. The chain itself may have stretched, the tensioner may be faulty or there may be a problem with low oil pressure.

However, the 1,493cc engines in later Spitfires have their own problems. Poor running when warm and misfiring under acceleration can often be traced to faulty waxstats in the carburettors. These engines are also more prone to overheating than the 1,147cc and 1,296cc types, and for that reason they may crack their cylinder heads. The symptoms – of water in the oil creating a frothy emulsion – are the same as those of a blown cylinder head gasket.

The engine is also probably the most

likely area in which to find non-original components. Even the most fastidious of owners would probably not have worried too much about the colour of his replacement distributor cap and plug leads, as long as they did the job and were cheap enough. The GT6 Mk 1 engine should have a chromed rocker cover, but in cases where the chrome has flaked off to a large degree some owners will have replaced it with the later painted type or simply stripped off the flaking chrome and painted over the whole cover to improve its appearance. Other items of this type, such as the correct air filter for each model of car, can be checked with the Thomason book recommended earlier.

THE TRANSMISSION

The gearboxes on these cars all have a reasonably clean bill of health, although naturally high mileages do take their toll. The most likely problems will be worn synchromesh (which reveals itself in the crashing of gears and the impossibility of making a 'clean' gear change) and jumping out of gear (usually most obvious when reversing). The Marina-type gearbox on the Mk IV and the 1500 Spitfire is rather more robust than the earlier types and has better synchromesh.

On cars fitted with overdrive you should always check that the overdrive does, in fact, engage and disengage properly. Sticking overdrive solenoids are not uncommon, although more than one apparently dead overdrive has been resurrected when someone reconnected electrical connections which had fallen off! The earlier D-type overdrive can be slow to engage at the best of times, so the absence of an instantaneous response should not lead you to think that there is a problem.

Two other common transmission problems are worth bearing in mind. First, apparently untraceable vibrations in the body, most commonly on Spitfires, can often be traced to a poorly-balanced propshaft or a worn UJ. Secondly, GT6s sometimes suffer from a curious rear-end rumble on the over-run, which as often as not is the result of wear in the differential.

THE SUSPENSION

Unless the car you are looking at has had a recent and thorough suspension overhaul, it is likely to rattle and creak as it runs over bumps and hollows in the road. This is quite normal, but, of course, the fewer rattles and creaks there are, the less work will need to be done. Attention to the suspension, in particular, by replacing its bushes, can utterly transform the way a car feels and can remove all the unwelcome noises from down below.

The front suspension on all Spitfire and GT6 models shares the same coil spring and double wishbone design. It is a neat and compact installation which has found its way into several component cars and even racing machinery, but it does need to be maintained properly if trouble is to be avoided.

The threaded trunnion on the vertical link or kingpin may fail in bad cases of neglect, and the front wheel will simply collapse into the wheelarch. To check for impending trouble, jack the car up, grasp each front wheel in turn at 12 o'clock and 6 o'clock and then try to rock it. Any movement between the lower wishbone and the trunnion indicates a degree of wear and the trunnion bushes should then be replaced as soon as possible. This is not an expensive job and is far cheaper than waiting until the bolt hole in the wishbone has worn oval, when the whole wishbone will have to be replaced. If things are left even longer, the wheel will collapse and may cause even more expensive damage – as well as a traffic accident.

Vibration felt through the steering wheel will probably not be caused by worn trunnions. It is more likely to result from worn wheel bearings, a worn steering rack or perhaps wheels and tyres which are out of balance.

Although there are several varieties of rear suspension, all of them share the same basic principle of a single, transverse, leaf spring. The spring itself does not normally give trouble, although there may be a certain amount of sag after high mileages. In extreme cases, leaves can break, but if this has occurred it suggests that the car has been neglected, abused or both – so that you may well then decide not to buy it. Remember that the rear wheels do lean in markedly at the top on all models with the 'swing-spring' suspension (Mk IV and 1500 Spitfires and the final Mk 3 GT6s) and that this is not an indication of a broken spring.

The earlier Spitfires and GT6s were notorious for the breakaway oversteer which could occur under hard cornering, and the cause of it was the rear suspension design. If the rear suspension bushes or dampers are worn the handling is likely to be even more unpredictable. So these areas do deserve a careful check, and it is probably worth budgeting for early replacements unless you are absolutely sure that recent work has been done here to restore the suspension to its peak health.

The Mk 2 and later GT6s have a rear suspension which incorporates Rotoflex couplings and these deserve a special examination. The Rotoflex couplings are the large, rubber 'doughnuts' at the outer ends of the driveshafts and they are subjected to a good deal of wear and tear. As a

result, sooner or later they will show signs of wear. Look for signs of fatigue around the bolt holes and for the rubber segments starting to separate from the metal plates. Replacement of the couplings is not expensive but it is a time-consuming job.

Wheels may not strictly be part of the suspension but it is worth considering them here. Originality matters to many people, and if you are unsure whether the wheels on your car are the right ones, do check in Thomason's book. Loose, bent or damaged spokes in wire wheels tell their own story, but the other check to make is that there are no knocking noises from the centre-lock types. If there are such noises the chances are that the splines on the wheel will be worn and that urgent replacement will be needed. You are more likely to encounter this problem on the rear wheels (which, of course, transmit the power to the road) than on the undriven front wheels.

THE CHASSIS FRAME

The separate-chassis construction of these cars was anachronistic for the 1960s, by which time almost every competitor had gone over to monocoque construction. The backbone chassis tends to flex a little, and so a Spitfire or a GT6 may not feel as taut on the road as some of its contemporaries. This impression is naturally more acute in the open cars.

Many cars are likely to have some rust in their chassis outriggers, and the most vulnerable ones are those at the front which carry the bonnet pivot points. The outriggers under the footwells sometimes rust at their junction with the main chassis rails; but the other outriggers do not often rust. In any case, rusty outriggers need not be of major concern. Even in bad cases it is easy enough to replace them. Serious rust may have travelled from an outrigger into the bodyshell and you should be aware that it may be very difficult indeed to repair the body around its mounting points.

The main chassis rails do not often give trouble, but they may rust and they may be distorted or cracked on a car which has been involved in an accident. To repair a twisted chassis may be difficult and consequently expensive, and at present replacement is not an option because new chassis are simply not available. In old and tired cars the chassis frame may actually sag in the middle, and this may be what has happened if the doors refuse to shut cleanly and there is no other obvious cause. Make a special check for rust in the frame where the differential mounts to it, because

bad corrosion here may be impossible to repair.

SUPPORT

You still want a Spitfire or GT6? Whichever you choose there is a strong case for joining one of the enthusiasts' clubs. These are not reserved for the fanatical owners of cars in pristine condition but are a source of support and advice in the everyday maintenance, repair and general use of Spitfires and GT6s. More important still is that they are the *only* source of such information since the Triumph company no longer exists and the Rover Group garages which inherited its mantle usually do not want to

Not sure what you are buying? Then check the commission number – found on this bulkhead-mounted plate – against the list given in the appropriate chapter of this book.

know about cars manufactured before the middle of the 1980s. Clubs will put you in touch with other owners who share the same problems and with owners who may have solved them. They will give you the best possible understanding of the market for spares and will help you to locate specialists if you need them. Club members also have a keen eye for good and bad specialists and will not hesitate to make recommendations or warn of poor workmanship.

So, here are the addresses of the principal clubs dealing with the Spitfire and the GT6. Remember that addresses do change and so it will be advisable to check in the classic-car press if you are reading this at a date much later than when it was written (1999). Remember, too, that if you want a reply when writing to club officials you should enclose a stamped addressed envelope with your letter.

In the United Kingdom the largest one-make club is Club Triumph, which, as its name indicates, caters for all varieties of Triumph and not just for the Spitfire and GT6 models. This club issues a magazine and a newsletter and arranges discounts for members with a number of specialist firms. It can be contacted through its Membership Secretary at:

Club Triumph,
Freepost (SWB 20389),
Christchurch BH23 4ZZ
telephone/fax: 01425-274193
The club also has its own Internet site at:
www:http://ourworld.compuserve.com/hom
epages/triumph

There is also the Triumph Sports Six Club, which caters for all the separate-chassis models of the Herald family: the Herald, Vitesse, Spitfire and GT6. It has its own permanent headquarters and issues both a

well-produced monthly magazine, *The Courier,* and a quarterly magazine, *Turning Circle.* There are three separate registers which will be of interest to readers of this book. One covers the first three marks of the Spitfire, the second covers the Mk IV and the 1500 models, and the third covers all the GT6 types. You can contact the club at:

Triumph Sports Six Club Ltd,
Main Street,
Lubenham,
Market Harborough, LE16 9TF
telephone: 01858-434424
fax: 01858-431936

The situation is rather different in the USA, where the sheer size of the country means that club activity tends to be centred on geographical regions rather than on individual models. The Vintage Triumph Register covers all models of Triumph, but within it the Spitfire and the GT6 have their own consultant or co-ordinator. At the time of writing, he was:

David Pelham,
1900 Fairway Drive,
Springfield,
Illinois 62704,
USA

These two Triumph models also sold strongly in Australia, and it is no surprise to find that they have a strong following there. As in the USA, so in Australia: the size of the country makes it impracticable to focus club activities on individual models and so most activities are regional. The umbrella organization in Australia is the Triumph Sports Owners Association (TSOA), and regional contacts are listed in South Australia and in Western Australia. These are:

TSOA,
PO Box 192,
Glenside,
South Australia 5065

and

TSOA,
PO Box 147,
Nedlands,
Western Australia 6009

Finally, there is also a bimonthly, commercially-produced magazine devoted solely to the Triumph marque, which serves as a focus of interest and is available in most countries where there is a strong following. This is *Triumph World,* and in case of difficulty it can be obtained from its publishers:

CH Publications Ltd,
PO Box 75,
Tadworth,
Surrey KT20 7XF

There is also a contact address in the USA:
202 US Highway 22,
Green Brook,
New Jersey 08812,
USA

Index